100 YEARS OF ELECTRIC TRACTION

Colin J. Marsden

Plate 1: The Class 87 locomotives, introduced in the mid-1970s, are some of the most modern 25kV electric locomotives. In May 1984, two machines, Nos. 87006 *City of Glasgow* and 87012 *Coeur de Lion*, were painted by their home depot, Willesden, in new colours. No. 87012 emerged in executive two-tone grey and No. 87006 in all-over dark grey. The two machines are seen outside Willesden Depot, on 11th May 1984, prior to their entry into service. No. 87006 was later repainted into executive colours.

Colin J. Marsden

Oxford Publishing Company

Copyright © 1985 Oxford Publishing Co. and Colin J. Marsden

ISBN 0-86093-325-3

Typesetting by:
Aquarius Typesetting Services, New Milton, Hants.

Printed in Great Britain by:
Netherwood Dalton & Co., Huddersfield, Yorks.

Published by:
Oxford Publishing Co.
Link House
West Street
POOLE, Dorset

Plate 3 (right): One of the most infamous electrified lines in the country must surely be the Woodhead route, powered during 1951-4 using the 1,500 volt d.c. overhead system. Approaching Dunford Bridge, the highest point on the line, Class 76 locomotives, Nos. 76006 and 76024, head the 11.18 Monckton to Northwich Class 8 freight on 16th June 1981, a few weeks prior to the final closure of the line during the following month.

Paul D. Shannon

Plate 2 (above): The Southern Railway were the proud owners of three straight electric locomotives from the mid-1940s, which were normally in use on the Central Section on Newhaven boat trains. No. 20003, in pristine condition, stands at Brighton on 1st October 1948.

British Rail

INTRODUCTION

The study of electric rail traction is, to say the least, a complex subject. It can be traced back as far as 1842 when an experiment using a battery-powered 'locomotive' was tried on the Glasgow to Edinburgh route; the power unit — which could move only 7 tons — was capable of travelling at just 4m.p.h.

The first major breakthrough in electric propulsion came in 1879 at the Berlin Trades Exhibition when a 300 yard long track equipped with a centre third rail charged at 150 volts, powered a 3hp motor in a small locomotive. By 1882, a similar machine was used at Crystal Palace, operating with a train intermittently for over two years. The next step in development came in 1883 when Magnus Volk constructed a ¼ mile third rail system in Brighton from The Aquarium to Chain Pier. The railway was of 2ft. gauge and used small 4-wheeled power passenger cars, electric power being supplied by a dynamo driven by a 2hp gas engine. Such was the excitement about the Volk's system that great crowds visited the site each weekend, and queuing to travel on the line was quite commonplace. Originally, Brighton Corporation only granted Volk an operational licence for six months, but this was soon extended, with the line still operating today — albeit now owned by Brighton Corporation. After a short period the Volk's system was altered to 2ft. 8½in. gauge and extended to 1¾ miles in length.

In 1890, the first major step came in bringing electric traction to London, when the City & South London Railway commenced electric operation from King William Street to Stockwell using the third rail system. Some three years later the Liverpool Overhead Railway opened its doors. These small beginnings in electric traction, paved the way for a number of other systems to be introduced around the turn of the century, for example Waterloo to Bank (1898), the District Railway (1900), the Central London Railway (1900), Liverpool to Southport (1904) and the Newcastle to Tyneside system (1904).

From the early 1900s electric traction has constantly developed from applications on suburban lines, freight lines, and eventually on to main lines as we see it today. Most of the original systems used direct current (d.c.) equipment, normally at voltages of between 200-1,500. By 1904 some of the developing systems adopted the higher voltage alternating current (a.c.) system, as it was considered more suitable for rail traction purposes. The first line to introduce this a.c. system was the Lancaster—Morecambe—Heysham route, which commenced using 6,600 volt 25 cycle a.c. in 1908. Of course, with a.c. it was not practical to have ground level pick-up, so an 'overhead' catenary system was developed with the power line being suspended over the track, current being collected by the train via a bow or pantograph. The catenary — bow/pantograph system was also used on some d.c. lines where the presence of a third rail was not conducive to good operating. Another major user of the a.c. system was the London, Brighton & South Coast Railway, who obtained authority to install a 6,700 volt a.c. system on most of its routes in 1903, but lines in the suburban area (to where the system was eventually confined) did not commence operation until 1909.

Although the LB&SCR a.c. system was quite successful, by the time it became established the other 'Southern' companies had adopted the outside third rail d.c. system, and the, by then, Southern Railway decided that this sore thumb network should be re-equipped for d.c. operation.

Between 1914 and 1922 a couple of adventurous projects were instigated by the North Eastern Railway. The first was in 1914/16 when the Newport to Shildon line was electrified for freight operation; the second projected scheme which never came to fruition was the electrification of the main line between York and Newcastle at 1,500 volt d.c. overhead; however a prototype locomotive was constructed and used for test purposes on the Newport line.

In the years that followed, a number of electrically-propelled systems were introduced on both the major company routes, and some on minor railways alike. Considerable technical development was made in both d.c. and a.c. power types over the years, and the railways of Britain, today, still use both systems, but it would be unlikely for any 'new' routes to be constructed on the third rail system alone.

In recent years major advancement has been made in electronics and a number of electric multiple units and locomotives have included highly sophisticated control principles, and automatic operation for the main line is only just around the corner.

This volume, *100 Years of Electric Traction* traces the history of the main and suburban systems of British Railways and its constituent companies. Mention is made, and pictorial coverage is given, to other systems such as Volk's Electric Tramway and the London Underground etc., who were also pioneers in electric propulsion in Great Britain. The book is divided into a number of parts which divide again into groups, or types, and these are again split into individual fleets or classes, having its own page(s) headed by a brief description and followed by photographs. Some types/classes may have only one illustration whilst others have several, this being dictated by the amount of space and the number of suitable illustrations available which show relevant development/changes to the stock. Towards the end of the book small sections have been devoted to London Transport, the Tyne & Wear Metro, the Glasgow Underground and other small electric systems. Individual books could quite easily be written about all of these in their own right, but to give a full coverage of the electric railways in this country these have been included.

I would like to record my thanks to a number of people who have assisted in the preparation of this book, and especially Mr M. Scott and Mrs C. Finnigan of GEC Traction Ltd., Mr J. N. Faulkner and Mr M. Collins for spending many hours researching and writing some of the heading articles, Mr D. Mercer for printing most of the black and white illustrations, Mrs J. W. Marsden for typing the manuscript and captions and, lastly, the publishers for allowing me complete freedom in content, selection, and layout of this book. It is hoped that readers of *100 Years of Electric Traction* will find it as interesting to read and browse through, as it has been to write and edit.

Colin J. Marsden
Surbiton
May 1985

Plate 4 (left): As this book went to press, British Rail sought tenders for a new design of electric locomotive called 'Electra', with a top speed of around 140m.p.h. It is envisaged that providing a successful tender becomes available, the first locomotive could be operational in 1989. This picture shows a model of how 'Electra' might look.

BR Board

CONTENTS

PART 1 — ELECTRIC MULTIPLE UNIT TRACTION

Section A : SR/BR (S)

1898 Waterloo & City Stock

One of the first applications of electric rail traction in England came in 1898 when the London City extension line, or the Waterloo & City Railway, was opened, the line being electrified by the side-contact third rail system, with power supplied by the line's own steam-driven generators at the Waterloo end. After 1915 power was taken from a surface powerhouse near Waterloo main line station. Stock for the 1 mile 46 chain line was ordered from Jackson & Sharp of Wilmington, USA. The vehicles were not actually constructed in America but were shipped to England in sections and assembled at the railway workshops at Eastleigh. Each 'train' consisted of four vehicles; a single-ended motor driving car at each end with two trailer cars between. Passenger accommodation was spartan, with wooden seating, only the very minimum of lighting and ventilation, and no heat. The driving cabs were equally basic with only the essential controls and a wooden stool seat. With the opening of the line on 8th August 1898, five of the American four car trains were required to operate every five minutes throughout the day, seven days a week. By 1899 it was decided that four car trains were uneconomic to operate in 'off peak' periods, and so five double cab single car motor vehicles were ordered from Dick, Kerr & Company of Preston, and these were delivered later the same year. By the early 1900s the line had become popular with City travellers, and two additional trailer vehicles were constructed by the Electric Tramway Company of Preston to act as spares. In 1922 the LSWR works at Eastleigh built a further four trailers to augment the original four car USA sets. All the original Waterloo & City cars were of wooden construction and were finished in a dark brown livery, maintenance being undertaken at Waterloo.

In the mid-1920s a train identification system was introduced with the 5 five car sets each being allocated a letter A-E. This coding system is still in operation today and assists the identification of sets during peak periods.

The traction equipment on original power cars consisted of two directly-wound armatures on the axles of one bogie, developing some 120b.h.p. This basic and early use of electric propulsion in rail application remained in use until 1940 when the line was refurbished with new stock, and all the original cars were scrapped.

Numbering applied to original Waterloo & City cars:

1 -12	1898 Jackson & Sharp single-ended motor cars.
13-17	1899 Dick, Kerr double-ended motor cars.
21-30	1898 Jackson & Sharp trailer cars.
31-32	1904 Electric Tramway Company trailers.
33-36	LSWR trailer cars.

Plate 5 (left): Dick, Kerr built double-ended Waterloo & City Railway motor car No. 15, introduced in 1899, a year after the line opened. In this photograph it stands alone at Waterloo during the 1930s. The main power bogie is at the near end.

Author's Collection

Plate 6 (right): The interior of the leading end of an original Waterloo & City motor coach. Note the wooden seating with hardly any apparent lighting, and also no heat. In this view, the door to the motorman's compartment is open.

GEC Traction Ltd.

SL, CP and CW Overhead Stock

During the early years of the 20th century, the London, Brighton & South Coast Railway sought powers to electrify its network and received authority to do so in 1903. It was decided to use a 6,700 volt a.c. system, voltage being collected by trains via roof-mounted 'bow' collectors. By the end of that year a decision was made for the South London line, between Victoria and London Bridge, to be the first section to be electrified. Rolling stock for the scheme was provided by eight three car trains constructed by the Metropolitan Amalgamated Carriage & Wagon Company, each consisting of a third class driving motor brake at each end, with a first class trailer between. The external appearance was very smart, with wooden panelling painted in umber brown and cream. Traction equipment was two 115hp Winter Eichberg motors carried under each driving cab.

Public service commenced in December 1909, but after a few months it became apparent that alterations would have to be made to passenger accommodation as far too many seats were provided in 'off peak' periods, and the number of first class seats invariably outweighed the demand. Therefore, by the end of 1910, the first class cars were removed for use as locomotive-hauled vehicles, and a new fleet of driving trailers were converted and coupled to the original driving motor vehicles, making a fleet of sixteen two car units.

The LB&SCR Board soon declared the electrification a total success, and proposed extensions to the system. The next line to be electrified was the Victoria/London Bridge to Crystal Palace, via Streatham Hill, section. Stock for this route was provided by thirty motor coaches and thirty driving trailers which were constructed by the Metropolitan Amalgamated Carriage & Wagon Company, together with a further thirty driving trailer vehicles constructed by the LB&SCR at Lancing. The livery was umber brown but the finish was not as ornate as the South London stock as much of the fine coach detail was omitted.

By 1913 several further projected extensions to the electrified system were planned but, regretfully, due to the outbreak of world hostilities in 1914 most of the scheme was shelved. After the end of the war, in 1918, it was agreed that finance could again be directed to electrification and the line to Brighton and Eastbourne was chosen, but as time progressed only the section to Coulsdon (North) and Sutton was electrified and opened to the public in April 1925. Rolling stock for the Coulsdon/Sutton lines consisted of twenty one motor vans (which received the name 'milk vans'), sixty driving trailers and twenty ordinary trailer vehicles. The twenty one motor vans were quite unusual, basically being an electric locomotive with a driving position at each end and a guard's compartment in the middle. These vehicles were built by the Metropolitan Carriage, Wagon & Finance Company of Birmingham.

When introduced, trains on the Coulsdon (North) route were usually formed into five car formations — driving trailer third class, composite driving trailer, third class, motor van, composite trailer and a third class driving trailer. Trains were usually formed as one five car set, but during peak hours two units operated in multiple. On introduction, livery was LB&SCR umber and cream, but this changed to green on formation of the Southern Railway.

After 1926 the stock was classified into three types: SL — South London stock; CP — Crystal Palace stock; CW — Coulsdon and Wallington stock. Regretfully, as most of the Southern Railway was adopting the third rail electric system, the 'overhead' routes soon became a sore thumb to the SR Board and a decision was made, in August 1926, to convert the overhead network to third rail operation. Overhead lines started to close from June 1928 when the London Bridge/Victoria to Streatham Hill and Crystal Palace line was converted, and this was followed by the other routes in September 1929. A number of original vehicles were rebuilt into third rail electrics, but the 'milk vans' were converted into goods brakes at Eastleigh.

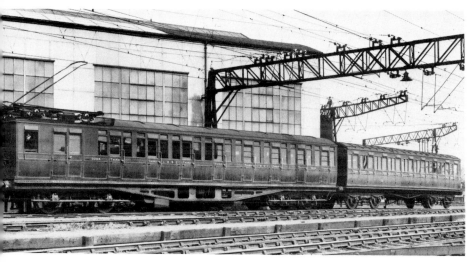

Plate 7 (left): The main servicing and repair facility for the LBSCR overhead stock was at Peckham Rye, where SR stock maintenance was undertaken for a number of years after the a.c. system was abolished. Standing outside the shed a South London line two car set, formed of motor car No. 3204 and driving trailer No. 4057, was photographed in the early 1920s.

Author's Collection

Plate 8 (right): For the 1925 extension of the 'Elevated Electric Railway' a fleet of twenty one motor vans (which became known as milk vans) was introduced, built by the Metropolitan Carriage Wagon & Finance Company. These vehicles were basically locomotives as they incorporated a driving position at each end, with guard's accommodation in the middle. No. 10101 is illustrated when new.

GEC Traction Ltd.

LSWR Motor Sets

In 1913 the London South Western Railway (LSWR) announced their intention to undertake electrification of their suburban routes from Waterloo to Wimbledon, Kingston, Shepperton, Hampton Court, the Hounslow Loop line and both main and Cobham routes to Guildford. Stock for this scheme comprised 84 three coach sets which were built at the LSWR workshops at Eastleigh and allocated numbers E1-E84. Each set was made up of two driving motor brakes with a trailer between. Traction equipment producing 1,100hp was provided by two motors mounted under the driving cabs. Electrical equipment was supplied by the Westinghouse Company, and the main control equipment was housed in a small compartment behind the driving cab.

Power for the LSWR electrified system was provided by an outside third rail, current being transferred to the stock by slipper shoes, one mounted at each corner of the unit on a beam supported by the bogie. Before the LSWR could embark on its electric railway, a powerhouse had to be built to provide current for the third rail. This was constructed at Durnsford Road, near Wimbledon, and was completed in 1915. The first three car motor set entered service from 25th October 1915 on the Waterloo to Wimbledon, via East Putney, section. Services on the Kingston and Shepperton lines followed in January 1916, with the other lines being completed shortly after. Again, the war years intervened and no extension to the electrifed system was possible for some years, until hostilities ended and finances were again available.

The 84 motor sets were rebuilt at Eastleigh Works from 1904 vintage steam-hauled suburban sets, mounted on wooden underframes. The cab ends were shaped in a 'torpedo' style and incorporated two windows, with a central headcode box where a letter stencil code was displayed to identify the required route. Accommodation was provided for both first and third class passengers with a total of 185 seats in a three car set. The units were allocated to a new electric depot at Wimbledon, adjacent to Durnsford Road Power-Station, where all regular maintenance was carried out.

After the railway Grouping in 1923, the stock was renumbered into the 1201-84 series, and operated alongside the later three car suburban units. In the following years, the majority of original motor sets were augmented with additional trailers and classified as 4SUB (four car suburban) sets. During the mid-1920s the units were repainted in Southern Railway green and remained in operation for many years.

Plate 9 :   Two LSWR three car motor sets depart from East Putney Tunnel during October 1916 with a Waterloo to Wimbledon, via East Putney, train. A total of 84 of these three car motor sets was constructed at Eastleigh, all out of 1904-built suburban stock.

British Rail

3SUB and Trailer Sets

3SUB

The 3SUB or three coach suburban unit dates from 1925 when the Southern Railway introduced a fleet of 55 sets on the Western and Eastern Sections. Of the original order, there were two distinct batches; the first 26, numbered 1285-1310, were mounted on short frames, whereas those built for the Eastern Section were mounted on standard length frames and numbered 1496-1524. On Western Section sets seating was provided for 48 first and 170 third class passengers, whereas Eastern Section sets, being slightly longer, accommodated 56 first and 180 third class passengers. Vehicles were constructed by the Metropolitan Vickers Ltd.

These three car units proved highly successful, and further sets, numbered 1401-95 and 1525-34, were introduced in 1926 for use on the Eastern Section. These batches were not 'new builds' but were converts from former SECR steam stock, conversion to electric taking place at Ashford Works.

During the 1927-34 period several further batches of 3SUB units emerged, the majority again being conversions from steam-hauled vehicles, but as these came from a number of sources, several detail differences existed.

After some years the Southern Railway decided that fixed four coach trains would be more beneficial to operate, and during the 1940s, a start was made to alter three car units to four. This was done by adding another trailer vehicle. Some were steam stock rebuilds, previously in use as part of trailer sets, whilst others were of new construction.

The last 3SUB stock operated during 1949, mainly on the South Western Hounslow Loop line where platform lengths were unable to accommodate more than six car formations. Of the original 3SUB units No. 1782 is worthy of mention, as it remained in service for many years as a CM&EE instruction unit carrying the number S10, which was later changed to 053.

TRAILER SETS

During the early 1920s passenger returns on the South Western electrified lines out of Waterloo required a revision of the service, with either additional trains being supplied or additional coaches added to existing services. The latter option was accepted, and a fleet of 24 two coach unpowered trailer sets was introduced, being converted from steam-hauled stock at Eastleigh Works. The trailer sets did not have driving positions, but on the outer ends air connections and electrical jumper cables were provided at a compatible height to the suburban electric multiple unit fleet. After the initial 24 sets were in service, further batches were introduced, all being converted from steam-hauled vehicles, and they were used on all three SR sections.

During the mid-1930s a considerable reorganisation of trailer sets took place, most being reformed to give better passenger loading, with some of the older vehicles being withdrawn. In the closing 1930s other trailer sets were withdrawn, some going for scrap, while others were again rebuilt and used as additional trailers to augment 3SUB units to four coach sets.

Plate 10 (above left): Following the implementation of the third rail electrification system throughout the Southern suburban area, several batches of 3SUB units were constructed; some were 'new build' vehicles while others were steam-hauled converts. Set No. 1528, introduced in 1926 for the Eastern Section, is seen near Otford in the early 1940s.

British Rail

Plate 11 (above right): This rare illustration shows a train of 1925-built a.c. overhead stock and a 3SUB unit, No. 1560, side by side in the carriage sidings at Coulsdon North during the mid-1920s. The doors of the 3SUB unit all carry class identification, and the trailer has accommodation for both first and third class passengers.

H. C. Casserley

Plate 12 (left): Trailer sets started to appear in the early 1920s to augment trains formed of two three coach suburban units. The trailer sets were rebuilt from steam-hauled vehicles and fitted with waist height air and power/control jumpers, enabling the power units to operate in multiple.

H. C. Hughes

2SL and 2WIM

The two car South London, and two car Wimbledon to West Croydon sets were rebuilds from former a.c. overhead stock. Eight 2SL units were converted from 16 a.c. driving cars at Peckham Rye Carriage Shops for use on the South London line between London Bridge and Victoria. The units were formed of a driving motor and a driving trailer, with all power and control equipment being housed in the motor vehicle. Seven third class compartments were provided in driving motor vehicles with a side corridor. Trailer vehicles were arranged for six third class and two first class compartments, also with a side gangway. The total seating capacity on a two car unit was for 16 first and 108 third class passengers.

The units commenced operation from May 1929 and carried the numbers 1901-1908, but these were altered during 1934 to 1801-1808 to avoid a number clash with other classes. The sets remained in service on the dedicated route, rarely straying elsewhere until their replacement in 1950, with the final unit being withdrawn in September 1954.

The 2WIM fleet consisted of just four two car units, which were re-built from eight first class trailers of 1908/9 South London line stock. These carriages had an interesting career; they were first introduced in 1908/9 as trailers to the original SLL stock. When the formations were revised in 1910, the cars became spare and were used as locomotive-hauled vehicles on the Brighton main line. In 1929 they were taken to Peckham Rye Works and rebuilt into two car electric multiple units. One car of each pair was fitted with traction equipment under the newly-formed driving cab position. Passenger accommodation was thus provided: driving motor cars — seven third class compartments connected by a side corridor; driving trailer vehicles were arranged with two first and four third class compartments. Total seating was for 16 first and 91 third class passengers. The set numbers allocated upon conversion were 1909-12; these were amended in 1934 to 1809-12. The four sets were usually employed on the Wimbledon to West Croydon route, and made rare appearances on the South London line. Units were eventually withdrawn during the mid-1950s.

Plate 13 (right): Slowing for the Wandsworth Road stop on the South London line's Victoria to London Bridge route, 2SL unit No. 1805 forms a London Bridge bound train during the mid-1950s. The eight South London units were all rebuilt from redundant a.c. driving cars when the overhead system was abolished.

Lens of Sutton

Plate 14 (left): Departing from the fascinating station of Denmark Hill, 2SL unit No. 1801 heads for Victoria on 19th April 1953 with a South London line service. The lower cab roofs are where the a.c. pantographs were previously fitted. When introduced in May 1929, this unit was numbered 1901, but was renumbered in 1937 to avoid a number clash with new stock under construction.

R. C. Riley

4 LAV

Prior to 1930 the only electric multiple unit stock constructed had been for suburban operation, but during 1930 a batch of 33 four coach units was ordered for use on the Central Section main line between Victoria and Brighton/Worthing, operating semi-fast and stopping services.

The construction of vehicles was carried out by the Southern Railway at Lancing and Eastleigh, with the first unit emerging in mid-1931, and deliveries extending over an eighteen month period. The SR classification given to the units was 4LAV (four coach lavatory-fitted set). Their formation was motor brake third at each end, with a trailer composite lavatory and a trailer composite between. The motor brake third cars had a driving cab at the outer end with a guard's van behind. Passenger accommodation was provided in seven compartments. TCL vehicles were also laid out as compartment cars, with a side corridor feeding five first and three third class compartments, a toilet being provided at each end. The TC cars were set out in a similar manner to TCL vehicles, except that four third and five first class compartments were supplied, the total train seating being for 70 first and 204 third class passengers.

The underframes of the LAV stock were steel-fabricated, and the body framing was of hard wood skinned in steel plate. The unit ends resembled earlier suburban builds, and incorporated two windows with a central headcode position, multiple control, power and lighting jumpers being carried on the end. An interesting feature of the LAV fleet was that the guard's compartment and cab were slightly inset from the remainder of the body line, giving an immediate recognition factor. After construction, running trials were carried out on the Western Section, but the units were soon to be found operating on the main Brighton line where schedules of 60 minutes between Victoria and Brighton could be maintained.

In 1939 two further sets were constructed at Eastleigh and incorporated modified electrical equipment. The 4LAV fleet remained operating primarily on the London to Brighton/Worthing routes until withdrawal in 1969. The sets were painted, from new, in green livery, yellow warning ends being applied during the mid-1960s.

Plate 15 (below): The Southern-designed LAV units were of distinctive appearance with the cab and guard's van areas slightly recessed. Painted in BR green livery, No. 2927 approaches Hayward's Heath on 7th October 1961 with a Brighton to Victoria semi-fast train.

Colin Boocock

PUL and PAN

A fleet of 20 six coach main line units was introduced by the Southern Railway in 1932, each set incorporating one Pullman vehicle finished in the Pullman Car Company's brown and cream livery, unlike the rest of the unit which was in SR green. These units were destined for the London to Brighton/West Worthing routes, and were constructed by the railway workshops at Eastleigh, the Metropolitan-Cammell Carriage, Wagon & Finance Company and the Birmingham Railway Carriage & Wagon Company. The railway works also constructed the trailer cars, while the two private companies each built twenty driving motor vehicles.

Traction equipment was housed in the driving cars, mounted at each end, and consisted of four 225hp BTH traction motors. Associated power and control equipment was also carried under the driving cabs. Passenger accommodation was made up of 52 third class seats in the 2 + 2 configuration. The body was constructed of steel panelling over a lattice framework. Trailer vehicles were constructed of steel panelling over a hardwood frame. The internal layout of cars differed, each unit having one vehicle with eight third class compartments plus a coupé, and two cars having five first and three third class compartments, each trailer being provided with end toilets. The Pullman vehicles in the sets were provided at the Pullman Car Company's expense, the actual building being undertaken by the Metropolitan-Cammell Carriage, Wagon & Finance Company. Pullman passenger accommodation was for both first and third class occupation, with an adjoining pantry containing full cooking facilities. All Pullman cars carried women's names; a practice of the Pullman Car Company.

All the twenty-strong fleet entered service during 1932/3 and were numbered 2001-2020, subsequently altering to 3001-3020 in 1937; the SR classification for the units being 6PUL. The PUL stock usually operated singly or with PAN stock on Victoria to Brighton/West Worthing duties,

seldom straying on to other routes. The sets remained in operation until replaced by more modern stock during the 1960s. However, five Pullman cars saw further use when, in 1964, five 4RES units were reformed with a Pullman car replacing their restaurant vehicles. These units were reclassified 4PUL and operated on the Central Section, normally with PAN or COR stock.

With the electrification of the Eastbourne and Hastings routes in 1935, seventeen six car main line units, classified as 6PAN, (6 coach pantry) entered service. For these sets 34 driving cars, which incorporated traction equipment, were constructed jointly between the Metropolitan-Cammell Carriage, Wagon & Finance Company and the Birmingham Railway Carriage & Wagon Company. Trailer vehicles were constructed by the Southern Railway at Eastleigh Works.

The PAN sets were basically PUL units, but in place of the Pullman vehicle an additional first class trailer car was provided which incorporated a small pantry — used to provide only light refreshments.

One noticeable difference between PUL and PAN sets was in the window design. On the PAN stock there was a fixed window with 'Airstream' ventilation above, these being introduced in an attempt to give draught-free ventilation. The PAN units were numbered in the 2021-2037 series when introduced, but from 1937 they changed to 3021-3037. The PAN units operated on their intended route along with diagrams on the Brighton and West Worthing lines, often working in multiple with PUL or CITY sets.

Withdrawal of this type commenced in the mid-1960s, with the final units being replaced when CIG/BIG stock entered service. In 1965 several PAN coaches were reformed with PUL cars to form 6COR units, remaining in use until 1969.

Plate 16 (below): The twenty-strong 6PUL fleet emerged in 1932 from Metropolitan Cammell, Birmingham Railway Carriage & Wagon Company and the SR works at Eastleigh, for use on the London to Brighton/West Worthing route. When constructed, sets were painted in Southern lined green livery as depicted here on set No. 2019, later renumbered 3019.

British Rail

Plate 17 (above): The 6PUL units had an overall length of 399ft. with a tare weight of 26.6 tons; passenger accommodation was provided for 72 first and 236 third class customers. Set No. 3010, containing Pullman car *Daisy*, passes Aldrington Halt en route from Littlehampton to Victoria on 31st May 1961.

Colin Boocock

Plate 18 (below): A twelve car formation of PUL stock hurries the 16.45 Victoria to Eastbourne and Ore service on the Quarry line near Merstham on 10th May 1958. The PUL units remained in service until the mid-1960s when new CIG/BIG stock was introduced on London to South Coast workings.

John Scrace

6CITY

In addition to the twenty 6PUL units previously described, three further six car Pullman units were constructed and classified as 6CITY. These were basically of the same formation as the PUL set, but were intended for use on the London Bridge to Brighton route, where many first class passengers travelled daily from the South Coast to London and required a full meals service.

Seating on CITY sets differed slightly. The driving motor vehicles were again set out for third class occupation, but each of the three trailers was dedicated to first class patronage, each vehicle being arranged in seven compartments, and toilets were provided in all traction vehicles.

Manufacture and the supply of power equipment was identical to that for PUL stock. When introduced in the autumn of 1932 the CITY sets were numbered 2041-2043, subsequently being altered in 1937 to 3041-3043.

In line with the Pullman Car Company tradition, first class vehicles were given women's names, and those chosen for the CITY stock were *Gwladys*, *Olive* and *Ethel*. The sets were replaced during the 1960s when new purpose-built Brighton line stock was introduced.

Plate 19 (below): A twelve car set of CITY/PAN stock led by CITY unit No. 3043 incorporating Pullman car *Ethel*, nears Haywards Heath on 8th August 1955 with a London to Worthing/Littlehampton train. Unlike PUL sets the CITY stock was primarily for first class travellers, with only the driving motor vehicle available for third class patronage.

British Rail

5BEL

Probably the most famous SR electric multiple units have been the three five car 'Brighton Belle' sets — 5BEL. These units were built for the SR in 1932 by the Metropolitan-Cammell Carriage, Wagon & Finance Company, each vehicle being manufactured to Pullman standard and, when introduced, were the first all electric Pullman cars in the world. The sets were intended for a newly-scheduled fast service between Victoria and Brighton, dubbed 'The Southern Belle'. Although the sets were electric multiple units, they broke the previous design and closely followed Pullman Car Company stock, with inward opening passenger doors and traditional Pullman styling.

The formation of each five car train was; driving motor brake third, seating 48 passengers, a third class parlour car seating 56, two first class parlour cars, each seating 20 and another driving motor brake third, giving a total unit capacity for 48 first and 152 third class passengers.

One of the main criteria laid down when the vehicles were under construction was that they should be the finest units in service. Special attention, therefore, was given to passenger comfort and internal noise levels. Coach bodies were of all steel construction with floors insulated by cork. Between the inner panels of the side walls and the steel skin was a thick layer of 'insulwood'. When the trains emerged in the early 1930s they carried Pullman brown and cream livery and the Pullman Car Company's coat of arms on each vehicle. First class carriages were named after women, whilst third class cars carried numbers. The name

'Southern Belle' was given to the services operated by BEL units from their introduction, but during 1934 the service was revised and the name 'Brighton Belle' was applied.

Operation of BEL stock was usually confined to the Victoria to Brighton line, and often two units ran together leaving the third as a spare. Sometimes units operated in multiple with PUL or PAN stock, particularly if a BEL unit was under repair.

In 1941, the three units were taken out of service and stored, but were always kept in operational condition. Unfortunately, one unit received war damage and was returned to the builders in 1946 for renovation. After the cessation of hostilites the stock recommenced service on the Brighton main line and continued until 30th April 1972 when their final run took place, and the Pullman service was discontinued from the Brighton line.

During the mid-1960s, when most of the other Brighton main line stock was withdrawn, it was decided that there was still life left in the BEL stock and the three units passed through Eastleigh Works for a heavy overhaul, emerging in a BR blue/grey Pullman livery. Thankfully, the vehicles were not sold for scrap when withdrawn and a number are now preserved, or have been sold to private individuals who use them for refreshment purposes. When introduced the sets were numbered 2051-3, subsequently changing in 1937 to 3051-3.

Plate 20 (left): Few photographs have ever been taken that show all three BEL units in one picture. However, this view, just outside Brighton, was photographed on 24th July 1962 and does just that. Heading for the station, unit No. 3052 leads another, on the 19.00 Victoria service, while the third member of the fleet is seen adjacent to Preston Park Pullman Workshops.

Colin Boocock

Plate 21 (below): By the late 1960s, when most Brighton electric stock was up for retirement, the 5BEL units still had plenty of life left in them, so it was decided to update the stock at Eastleigh Works for another two year's service. When completed, units emerged in the blue-grey Pullman livery and carried the 'Brighton Belle' legend on their body sides and front end. Set No. 3053 was photographed outside Eastleigh Works during late 1969.

Colin Boocock

2BIL

To provide for semi-fast services on the London to Eastbourne electrification, ten two coach units emerged early in 1935. Each two coach set was formed of a driving motor brake third and a driving trailer composite, giving a seating capacity for 24 first and 88 third class passengers.

In common with unit building of that period, the construction of power cars was awarded to the Metropolitan-Cammell Carriage, Wagon & Finance Company, and Birmingham Railway Carriage & Wagon Company, with the trailer vehicles being built by the Southern Railway at Eastleigh Works. Vehicle construction was based on a steel frame with hardwood side supports plated in steel.

Internal layout of the BIL units followed previous Southern styling, with a guard's and luggage compartment behind the driving cab in the power car. Seven third class compartments were connected by a side corridor, and at the inner end of the coach was a toilet. Driving trailer cars were set out in four first and four third class compartments, again fed by a side corridor with a toilet at the inner end.

The initial ten units were numbered in the 1891-1900 series when constructed, but this was later amended to 2001-2010. A subsequent fleet of units of the same design was built at Eastleigh Works in 1936 for semi-fast services on the Waterloo to Portsmouth/Alton lines, and these were numbered 2011-2048. Further batches taking the numbering to 2116 emerged in 1937 for the Central Section's Portsmouth to Bognor Regis route, and the final batch, Nos 2117-2152, entered traffic in 1938 for the Waterloo to Reading line. Some of the later builds had slightly revised seating in the motor coach, where six first class compartments were laid out, together with a coupé. Other minor alterations on later builds were to power equipment and window frame design. When introduced, all units were painted in green livery, the majority remaining in this colour until their withdrawal in the early 1970s. Some sets that passed through works for classified overhauls during the late 1960s, emerged in rail blue livery with full yellow warning ends.

Plate 22 (left): For a number of years the 'Coastway' route was the regular stamping ground for BIL stock. No. 2100, unusually formed with an all-steel driving trailer following war damage, is seen on 15th March 1960 at Portsmouth & Southsea. Several BIL units acquired all steel vehicles in the late 1940s/early 1950s following either collision or war damage.

Colin Boocock

Plate 23 (right): Standing with its driving motor brake nearest the camera, unit No. 2053 waits at Christ's Hospital on 25th May 1958 with a Bognor Regis to Three Bridges local service. The nose-end equipment on these units consisted of power jumper, control jumper and train lighting jumper; air connections being positioned under the buffer beam.

John Scrace

2NOL

The 2NOL, or two coach non-lavatory suburban units, were introduced in 1934, and were converts from LSWR steam stock, rebuilding for electric operation taking place at Eastleigh Works. Each two coach unit was formed of a third class driving motor coach of the usual pattern — full width driving cab with a small guard's and luggage compartment behind, with seven third class compartments and a coupé; coupled to this was a driving trailer composite with three first and six third class compartments. Total accommodation was provided for 24 first and 135 third class passengers. Traction and control equipment was supplied by Metropolitan Vickers (MV) Ltd.

A total of 78 NOL units was ordered by the Southern Railway, and all had been delivered by late 1936. The first units entered service on the Brighton to West Worthing route and, as further sets emerged, their operating range spread to the Horsted Keynes (Bluebell) branch, in addition to the Seaford branch on the Central Division. Later units went to the Western Section, taking over services on the Waterloo to Windsor/Weybridge routes. The number series given to the NOL fleet was 1813-1890. All units operated normally until 1942, when a number were taken out of service to have their traction equipment isolated for use as temporary trailer sets, usually operating between 4SUB units. From 1943 most units were modified internally by having the third class coupé in the driving motor car removed, thus enlarging the guard's accommodation. After the war years, those sets converted for trailer use were returned to power units, and a major reorganisation of sets commenced. Units Nos. 1813-50 retained their first and third class accommodation and operated on the Central Section, while sets Nos. 1851-90 became third class only, primarily for use on the Waterloo to Windsor/Weybridge line.

The NOL fleet continued in operation until the mid-1950s when they were replaced by new stock. Many of the NOL set frames were taken to works and adapted for use on EPB/HAP builds of the period.

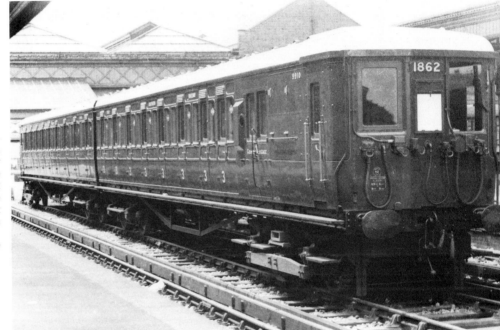

Plate 24 (right): The NOL non-lavatory suburban units were rebuilds of steam-hauled stock and, when first introduced, were destined for Central Section operation. Painted in the Southern Railway lined green livery, set No. 1862 is seen at Eastbourne during the 1930s. Note the class indication marked on the compartment doors, and the protruding guard's observation window on the side.

Colin J. Marsden Collection

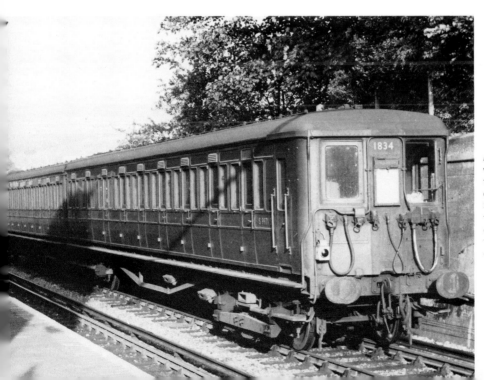

Plate 25 (left): Several alterations were made within the NOL fleets at various times but, by the late 1940s, the operating areas had settled down, with sets Nos. 1813-50 serving the Central Section and Nos. 1851-90 on the Western Section. Set No. 1834, retaining first and second class accommodation, stands at Lewes during the 1950s, with the DTC vehicle nearest to the camera.

J. H. Aston

4COR, 6COR, 4BUF, 4RES and 4GRI

COR, BUF.

With the London to Portsmouth electrification in 1937 came the delivery of new main line corridor stock, classified 4COR. These four coach sets were constructed by the SR at Eastleigh Works. The external design was a break from previous styling and incorporated a central gangway, with a train reporting number position on the opposite side to the driver's front window. The four car set formation was motor brake third open (MBTO), seating 52, trailer composite (TC), accommodating passengers in five first class and three third class compartments, third corridor (TK), with eight compartments and a coupé, and a further MBTO, toilet facilities being provided in both trailer cars. The inclusion of the corridor connections on set ends provided total freedom throughout an eight or twelve car train, when two or three sets were in multiple. It also gave passenger access to refreshment facilities, usually marshalled in the centre of a formation.

Traction equipment for the COR stock consisted of four 225hp traction motors, two mounted on the outer bogies of driving cars — these were supplied by Metropolitan Vickers Ltd. Numbers allocated to the original COR sets were 3101-3129. During 1937/8, a second identical batch of COR units entered service numbered 3130-3155 for use on the Mid-Sussex electrification scheme. Three further sets were introduced in the mid-1940s, numbered 3156-58, to replace damaged stock.

COR stock normally operated on the coastal-bound routes, usually in pairs, with a restaurant/buffet/griddle unit between. Following the introduction of new main line stock in the mid-1960s, the COR units were displaced to other duties, including the Coastway route and the Waterloo to Reading/Guildford line. Stock was finally withdrawn in September 1972. From 1964, the restaurant cars were removed from six 4RES and one 6PUL unit and, after reformation, seven 4COR(N) sets entered service numbered 3065-71 for use on the Littlehampton/Worthing routes. During late 1965, ten 6COR units were introduced, being formed of redundant PUL/PAN vehicles, and numbered 3041-50. Although classified as COR units, these sets were only fitted with gangways within sets, and did not have end corridor connections. Other reformations took place in 1965 and Nos. 3159-3168 were formed from redundant RES/PUL/PAN vehicles.

To operate with COR stock on the Waterloo to Portsmouth route, a fleet of thirteen buffet car sets was built at Eastleigh in 1938, and numbered 3073-3085. This batch of units was of similar design to the 4COR sets, but in place of the trailer third there was a buffet car, its internal layout consisting of a service compartment, bar with stool seats, and two toilets. The service section of the car contained all cooking facilities, and power for the buffet was provided by an underslung generator set. There are two points of interest about these sets. When built, the refreshment car was painted in Malachite green with the remainder of the unit in Brunswick green, and the bar was concave in shape.

RES, GRI.

To provide full restaurant facilites for the Portsmouth electrification, nineteen four car full restaurant sets, classified as 4RES, were introduced. Sets closely resembled the COR units which they operated alongside. The two driving motor vehicles, seating 52, were constructed by the SR at Eastleigh Works, whilst the third class trailer and the first class restaurant cars were built by the Birmingham Railway Carriage & Wagon Company Ltd., and the Metropolitan Carriage, Wagon & Finance Company respectively. The restaurant vehicle was set out in five compartments, each provided with four or six loose chairs, and a dining area with twelve additional seats. The third class trailer had a small pantry, kitchen and seating area for 36. After the RES stock entered service in 1937/8, they usually operated on their intended route, often sandwiched between two 4COR units. One of the RES sets is of special interest. On No. 3072 the restaurant car suffered considerable fire damage in 1952, and was subsequently rebuilt as a cafeteria style buffet car, the unit being reclassified as 4BUF.

RES stock remained in service until 1962, when three sets were taken out of service and rebuilt as griddle units; during modification work, the restaurant cars were completely rebuilt and accommodated a buffet, kitchen and bar sections. Units converted in this way became classified as 4GRI (four car griddle). Numbering which applied to RES sets was 3054-72, while those converted to GRI stock were renumbered 3086-88.

Plate 26 (below): One of the established and perhaps the most popular of the SR-designed electric multiple units were those of the COR, BUF, RES and GRI design, which all became affectionately known as 'Nelsons', mainly due to the headcode position on the opposite side to the driver's window, giving a 'one-eyed' effect. A 4COR/BUF/COR train passes Havant on 26th July 1958 with a Portsmouth Harbour to Waterloo service.

Colin Boocock

Plate 27 (above): Although the main stamping ground for COR units was the Waterloo to Portsmouth and Victoria to Bognor Regis routes, after new main line stock was introduced the units found other spheres of operation mainly on the Waterloo to Reading/Guildford and Brighton to Ore 'Coastway' routes. On a winter's night in 1969, set No. 3159 awaits departure from Brighton, bound for Ore.

John Vaughan

Plate 28 (below): In the later years of 'Nelson' units, the majority were outshopped in rail blue livery with full yellow ends. COR unit No. 3161, a set introduced in 1965 by reforming PUL/PAN/RES vehicles, leads another 4COR and a 4GRI set out of West Worthing with a London Bridge to Littlehampton duty during the summer of 1970.

John Vaughan

2HAL

This fleet of two coach main line non-corridor units, classified as HAL, with a lavatory fitted in one coach, was introduced from 1939 for use on the London to Maidstone/Gillingham electrification. Construction was carried out at Eastleigh Works from mid-1938, with the first deliveries being made in early 1939. The set formation was a driving motor third (DMT) fitted with a full width driving cab with guard's accommodation behind, together with seven third class compartments. Coupled to this was a driving trailer composite (DTC), set out in four first and four third class compartments together with a toilet, all being connected via a side corridor.

Power equipment housed under the DMT vehicle consisted of two 275hp English Electric traction motors fitted with electro-pneumatic control equipment. The original HAL stock was numbered in the series 2601-76. In late 1939 a further batch of sixteen units was built and numbered 2677-92, and these were identical in design to the 1938 build. During the war years several HAL and other unit types received damage.

Some were repaired but those seriously damaged were a total loss. Six HAL replacements were constructed at Eastleigh during 1948 and received the numbers 2693-99. These were different in external appearance and resembled the suburban (SUB) builds then under construction. The internal layout was also amended, with the DMT vehicle now having seven compartments connected via a side corridor. A final HAL, given the number 2700, emerged in 1955 and again differed internally. The DMT was now fitted with eight third class compartments connected by a centre gangway.

From their introduction until the late 1950s these units were on the Charing Cross to Gillingham/Maidstone route. However, following the introduction of new HAP stock, the HAL fleet was released to suburban and semi-fast services on all three operating divisions. When introduced, the HAL fleet was painted green, a livery in which most units remained. However, a few that underwent repairs in the late 1960s emerged in BR rail blue. Final withdrawal of the type took place in October 1971.

Plate 29 (below): After some overnight snow, 2HAL unit No. 2656 pulls through the deep Merstham Cutting, after emerging from Merstham Tunnel, with the 12.06 Victoria to Bognor Regis train, on 8th February 1969. A few HAL units which remained in service until the early 1970s returned to service from overhaul painted in rail blue livery with full yellow warning ends.

John Scrace

4SUB

By far the most numerous of the SR-designed multiple units were the 4SUB (four car suburban) units, first introduced in the early 1940s, when set No. 4101 was outshopped from Eastleigh Works. The set was formed of two driving motor thirds with two trailers between. The decision to introduce fixed four car formations was to remove the need to use trailer sets. At the same time as the first 4SUB emerged, it was announced that alterations to existing suburban stock would take place, resulting in the reformation of 3SUB units to four cars, the additional trailer, in most cases, coming from disbanded trailer sets.

Unit No. 4101 entered traffic in late 1941 on the Victoria to Orpington line. The seating layout was for 60 first and 396 third class passengers, the first class accommodation being provided in a trailer composite. However, it is unlikely that this accommodation was ever actually used for first class passengers, as it was dispensed with on suburban services from 6th October 1941. Over three years elapsed before the second 4SUB unit emerged from Eastleigh as No. 4102, in 1944. In 1945 production sets started to enter service with Nos. 4103-4110. By this time a vast number of 3SUB units were already in service, reformed as four car units, and thus renumbered in the 4XXX series. In 1946 Eastleigh constructed sets Nos. 4111-20, and these differed from previous 'new' SUB units by having wide compartment corridors in their motor cars. This was to accommodate the large numbers of standing passengers travelling in leading vehicles during peak periods. A further batch of identical units entered service in 1947/8 carrying numbers 4364-77. In 1946 sets Nos. 4121-30 entered service and again these were of a slightly revised layout, with coaches of a semi-open layout (three or four compartments grouped together with a gangway). After travelling in semi-open vehicles, passengers much preferred this internal design and pressure was brought upon the railway authorities to base future stock on this layout. In 1948/9, when sets Nos. 4277-99 entered traffic, these requirements had been honoured, with three of the four cars in an open design and this pattern continued on all subsequent builds. Nos. 4621-54 emerged in 1949 with Nos. 4655-4709 following in 1950, and Nos. 4710-4754 during 1951. After this, 'new' generation suburban stock, classified EPB, was introduced. Sets Nos. 4694-99, and 4718 were, when built, fitted with roller blind headcodes in place of the stencil type hitherto carried, serving as a prototype for future units. A number of the 3SUB/4SUB converts were phased out as 1949/51 builds entered service, and the majority had been withdrawn by the mid-1950s. A number of SUB car reformations took place over the years, resulting in several 'odd' sets. The SUB fleet remained largely intact until the first 'new' generation Class 508 electric multiple units were delivered from 1979, and subsequently Class 455 stock from 1982/3. The final SUB units remained in regular service until autumn 1983. When built, all units were painted in green livery, and those surviving after the corporate identity colours were introduced were painted in rail blue. Prior to the final demise of the SUB fleet, set No. 4732 was repainted by Selhurst Depot in SR green livery and sunshine lettering, and has been retained by BR for special duties.

Plate 30 (right): A wide variety of SUB unit styles have been built over the years, with a number of 3SUB sets being augmented into four coach units. This set, No. 4178, was formerly a 1658 type 3SUB unit, augmented by the addition of an ex-LSWR ten compartment trailer. Unit No. 4178, painted in early British Railways green livery with destination board on the brake van side, stands at Hampton Court during the early 1950s.

J. H. Aston

Plate 31 (left): All steel sets, constructed in the late 1940s and up to the end of 1951, have become known as the 'standard units'. All carried the same technical equipment and seated the same number of passengers. Set No. 4720, introduced in 1951, stands at New Cross Gate while an LTE unit and an 80000 Standard tank locomotive can be seen in the background.

J. H. Aston

Plate 32 (left): When sets Nos. 4694-99 and 4718 emerged from Eastleigh Works at the end of 1950 they were fitted with a roller blind headcode system, which served as prototype equipment for headcodes on the EPB sets. Set No. 4695 approaches Norwood Junction from Bromley Junction on 28th May 1960, painted in green livery. Note the warning whistle to the right of the driver's window.

Colin Boocock

Plate 33 (below): The SR would have preferred to have eliminated the SUB units by the end of the 1970s, however, due to prolonged delivery of replacement stock, SUB units remained in traffic until the autumn of 1983. Set No. 4630 passes under West London Junction signal box with a Twickenham to Waterloo, via Hounslow, service on 9th January 1982, during a heavy snowstorm.

Colin J. Marsden

Plate 34 (above): In recent years, SUB stock has only operated on the Central and Western Divisions, being allocated to Selhurst and East Wimbledon depots. Wimbledon-allocated No. 4666 leads a sister unit through Clapham Cutting on 3rd June 1981 with the 09.42 Waterloo to Dorking service.

Colin J. Marsden

Plate 35 (above): Although SUB stock was quite capable of main line operation, which was demonstrated on the rare occasion, sets were usually confined to suburban or local duties. Departing from Norwood Junction on 5th March 1982, No. 4678 heads a Victoria to Epsom Downs service.

Colin J. Marsden

Plate 36 (below): After the introduction of Classes 508 and 455 on the South Western Division, 4SUB units began to disappear, particularly during off-peak periods. Units Nos. 4678 and 4660 slowly depart from Barnes on 27th October 1982 with a Waterloo (Main) to Waterloo (Windsor), via Kingston, service.

Colin J. Marsden

4DD

During 1948, in the months prior to nationalisation, Mr O. V. S. Bulleid had plans drawn up for a double-deck or DD unit, based on the successful SUB design. The experimental type was to have accommodation on two levels, but unlike bus seats, were to be arranged in a 'high'-'low' configuration throughout the unit, access to the 'high' deck being by shallow steps.

Design plans were accepted, and the first complete unit emerged late in 1949. Once the four car set was operational, passenger reaction was gauged, and unfortunately it was unfavourable, as passengers soon filled the lower deck, and some even stood, whilst seats remained empty on the upper stage. The second of these units appeared early in 1950, and from then on the two usually operated together on the South Eastern Section on routes from Charing Cross to Dartford.

Each set had accommodation for 552 passengers, with room for about another 150 standing, set out as follows: Driving Motor Brake Third — 55 seats 'high' and 55 seats 'low'; Trailer Third — 66 seats 'high' and 78 seats 'low'. In addition, each car had ten tip-up seats on the 'high' level.

Although sets conformed basically to the SUB design, they were slightly larger, and therefore heavily restricted on their operating area. To permit the stock to conform to the loading gauge, no external stepboards were fitted. Power and control equipment was by English Electric, with traction motors being mounted on the outer ends of the driving cars. One advancement fitted on DD stock, from new, was strip lighting, greatly improving the interior illumination. Pressure ventilation was also an essential fitting, as no opening windows were placed in the upper areas. When constructed, the sets were painted in green livery and numbered 4001-2. When the sets passed through works, in the late 1960s, they emerged in BR rail blue and, from November 1970 were renumbered 4901-2, thus vacating their previous number series for new high density stock then on delivery.

The DD units remained in service on the Dartford routes until October 1971, when they were withdrawn. Regretfully most vehicles were scrapped, but two cars have successfully been preserved.

Plate 37 (below): The two unique DD or Double Decker units were heavily restricted on their operating routes, and were usually in service on the Charing Cross to Dartford, via Sidcup, line. Both units, led by set No. 4002, approach Dartford on 2nd October 1968 prior to the abolition of semaphore signalling in the area.

John Cooper-Smith

6TC and 7TC

For a number of years, the trailer control (TC) method of operation was considered by BR (Southern). The principle of the TC system was to have a 'set' formed of a number of unpowered coaches provided with a driving position at each end, acquiring the traction power from an outside source, such as a locomotive or another powered unit. The first TC stock entered service in 1963, when unit No. 900 emerged, formed of seven redundant electric multiple unit vehicles. The stock comprised the two driving cars of BIL No. 2006, four ten compartment trailers from various SUB units, and one trailer composite, rebuilt from a SUB trailer second. The seven car formation provided accommodation for 72 first and 604 second class passengers. Set No. 900, later renumbered 701, took up operation on the London Bridge to Tunbridge Wells (West), via Oxted, route from late 1963, normally working one 'up' and one 'down' service each day, with a Class 33 locomotive providing the power. Although this set was referred to as a TC, it was really only a set of trailer coaches, as it was unable to control a locomotive from its cabs.

The Southern Region decided to take the system one stage further when it was planned to marshal rakes of COR/PUL and PAN stock together, and form six coach TC sets for use on the Oxted line. As time proved, only one set was formed, No. 601, and this only operated for a short period on the intended route before being transferred to the twice daily Clapham Junction to Kensington Olympia duty. Accommodation on No. 601 was for 72 first and 264 second class passengers. To operate with No. 601, a Class 33 locomotive, No. D6580, was specially converted, and fitted with waist height air pipes and control jumpers, enabling traction control of the locomotive to be transferred to the remote cabs of the TC unit. This set could normally be found on the Clapham Junction to Kensington route until it was withdrawn in the early 1970s following collision damage. The TC and power principle was considerably developed with the eventual introduction of the REP/TC stock on the Bournemouth line in 1966/7.

Plate 38 (left): Of the two trailer control sets introduced, only No. 601, formed of COR/PUL/PAN stock, was able to operate a locomotive at its remote end. During conversion work, all powered bogies were replaced by the trailer type, and the end gangways were removed. No. 601 was photographed stabled at Clapham Junction during 1967, when the set was in regular operation on the Clapham Junction to Kensington Olympia service.

Colin Boocock

Plate 39 (right): Although the 7TC set retained its former driving positions and yellow warning ends, it was really a rake of trailer vehicles and had to be hauled at all times. The set is seen at Oatlands Sidings on 17th September 1967 whilst en route from Eastleigh Works to the Central Division.

R. E. Ruffell

2EPB and 4EPB

Towards the end of 1951, the first of a 'new' generation electric multiple unit emerged from Eastleigh Works, classified EPB. These units were direct descendants of the SUB fleet but new, modern, and in some cases novel ideas were included. Major differences between the EPB fleet and their predecessors was the fitting of electro-pneumatic (EP) brake equipment, and it is from this that the SR type code is derived. Other alterations included the fitting of a motor generator set to provide a 70 volt supply for control. Buckeye couplers were also fitted on unit ends, together with waist height air and control jumper cables.

Passenger accommodation was similar to the final SUB builds, and the formation of a four car set was thus: Motor Brake Third Open, Trailer Third Compartment, Trailer Third Open, Motor Brake Third Open. MBTO vehicles carried all power/control equipment, with traction motors mounted on the outer bogies. Seating was for 82 passengers in the MBTO and 112/120 in trailer vehicles. The first 4EPB set, carrying the number 5001, emerged in November 1951 and operated test trips on the Waterloo to Guildford, via Cobham, route. The pioneer unit was soon joined by others and, by the end of 1952, thirteen were in traffic. Several subsequent orders for the type were placed, and the production run eventually ran to over 200. Sets Nos. 5016-48 emerged in 1953 and Nos. 5049-53 in 1954. During 1953, sets numbered in the 51XX series commenced delivery, and these were the same as the 50XX units except for detail differences, mainly on the bogies. The final 4EPB unit emerged during 1957.

Upon completion of the initial 4EPB build, a fleet of 2EPB sets commenced delivery. These were formed of a Motor Brake Second Open, and a Driving Trailer Second. Cars were of the same general design as in the 4EPB units and each two car set accommodatd 178 passengers. The number series allocated was 5651-5684. These sets were built on reclaimed frames from 2NOL stock, and were introduced mainly for use on the Waterloo to Windsor/Weybridge line. However, in recent years, they have operated on the Central Division.

During the mid-1950s, the need was looming for additional suburban units, and the BR design team prepared plans for an 'updated' EPB, based on BR standard coach design. A fleet of 79 two coach BR-designed EPB units commenced delivery in 1954, primarily intended for the South Eastern Division. Although of BR design, they incorporated the earlier type control equipment. MBSO vehicles were equipped in the standard manner with full width driving cab, guard's compartment, and two four bay saloons to provide passenger accommodation. The Driving Trailer vehicle was arranged with a full width driving cab, together with five compartments and a four bay saloon, giving a total seating capacity for 186. In 1954/5, a further fifteen sets were constructed for the North Eastern Region's 'Tyneside Electrification' system. These sets resembled the BR-designed units of the period for the Southern Region except for a larger luggage van, thus reducing the passenger accommodation to one three and one four bay saloon. Headcode boxes were not carried, but in their place front marker lights and destination indicators were fitted. These sets operated on the North Eastern Region until 1963 when the system was de-electrified and the stock returned to the Southern for use alongside their EPB sets. By the late 1950s, further four car suburban sets were required, and orders were placed for a substantial fleet of BR-designed four car units closely resembling the BR two car sets of the mid-1950s. These four car units were set out as follows: MBSO, TS, TS, MBSO. The MBSO vehicles were laid out in two four bay saloons, whilst TS cars were of an unusual design, having five compartments and a five bay saloon. These units, numbered in the 53XX range, emerged during 1959/61 and were destined for operation on the South Eastern Division. During 1962/3, a further fleet of fourteen units emerged for South Western Division operation but, after only a short period, these were reallocated to the South Eastern Division.

During the mid-1970s, it was deemed that wholesale replacement of the SR electric multiple unit fleets would not be probable for many years, and so it was decided to facelift or refurbish many of the existing fleets. As a prototype for this move, two SR-designed HAP(SAP) sets were disbanded and reformed with spare trailer vehicles, to form a new EPB set, No. 5263, which passed through Eastleigh Works, and was rebuilt with lower ceiling, flourescent lighting, open layout coaches, and trimmed in modern decor. Upon release, the unit was much approved and, by 1979, a major facelift programme was authorised. Over sixty SR-designed 4EPB units received a facelift at Horwich and Eastleigh Works, which included an alteration to make all vehicles of open layout with improved lighting and internal decor. In addition to the EPB facelift programme, a number of SR-designed HAP (SAP) vehicles were also included and marshalled with rebuilt SUB trailers to form additional 4EPB units. At the end of 1982, further facelift schemes were authorised for SR-designed two car and BR-designed four car units. Again all vehicles were revised to the open layout and, under the TOPS classification, the EPB types became:

Original SR-designed 4EPB units	415/1
BR-designed 4EPB units	415/2
Facelifted SR-designed 4EPB units	415/4
Facelifted BR-designed 4EPB units	415/6
SR-designed 2EPB units	416/1
BR-designed 2EPB units	416/2
Facelifted SR 2EPB units	416/3

During 1985, the EPB fleets were allocated to all three operating divisions and should be represented for some years to come. A number of SR-designed units are, however, scheduled for early retirement.

Plate 40 (below): By the early 1950s, the SR-designed 4EPB units were taking over some inner and outer suburban duties. With an 'S' prefix, No. S5202, complete with a whistle above the driver's window, passes Vauxhall on 28th August 1959 with the 12.52 Waterloo to Guildford, via Cobham, service.

John Scrace

Plate 41 (above): A profile of a BR-designed 2EPB unit from the driving trailer end, distinguishable from the MBS vehicle by the omission of the guard's compartment. These sets, Nos. 5701-5779, accommodate 186 second class passengers and have a tare weight of 70 tons. Nose end equipment consists of air brake and main reservoir pipes, control jumper cable/socket, and power jumper socket.

British Rail

Plate 42 (left): One of the most important factors on the SR, who, during 1985, operated the largest electric multiple unit coaching stock fleet on BR, is maintenance. Each set is programmed to visit a depot most days for a check-up, with strict attention being paid to items such as bogies, traction equipment and brakes. BR-designed 4EPB unit No. 5320 and 4CEP unit No. 7140 stand inside Chart Leacon Depot, Ashford, during 1961.

British Rail

Plate 43 (above): When constructed, the EPB fleet was in green livery, but this progressively changed to rail blue during the 1970s. From 1979, units again changed colour with blue/grey livery being applied as units received classified attention. Set No. 5002 departs from the Central Section platforms at Clapham Junction during the summer of 1981 with a Victoria to Coulsdon North working.

Colin J. Marsden

Plate 44 (right): The EPB fleets of two car and four car units are currently allocated to all three divisions, with the South Eastern Division having by far the largest allocation. Departing from Putney, on 11th August 1981, 4EPB unit No. 5117 leads a two car BR-designed set with a Waterloo (W) to Waterloo (W), via Hounslow, working.

Colin J. Marsden

Plate 45 (left): The BR-designed EPB units with their slab style sides are easily identifiable from SR sets by either the unit ends or side window differences. BR 4EPB set No. 5324 leads 3 two car sets towards Crayford, on 29th May 1981, with a Charing Cross to Slade Green empty stock train.
Colin J. Marsden

Plate 46 (below left): All EPB units operated by the South Eastern Division are allocated to Slade Green Depot (SG). However, a number of smaller maintenance points carry out daily checks on stock. On 29th May 1981, set No. 5363 arrives at New Eltham with a Cannon Street to Gravesend.
Colin J. Marsden

Plate 47 (right): This illustration of a typical South Eastern Division ten coach EPB formation was taken during the transition period from blue to blue/grey livery. The train is headed by 2EPB (Class 416) unit No. 5723, and is a Gillingham to Cannon Street working, photographed at Higham.
Colin J. Marsden

Plate 48 (below): After heavy overnight snow, which is being whisked up by the train, a 2EPB/4VEP formation passes Wimbledon West Junction, on 11th January 1982, led by 2EPB unit No. 5787, an ex-Tyneside example, with a Waterloo to Woking stopping service. The EPB fleet is compatible with all stock built after 1951 except Class 455.

Colin J. Marsden

Plate 49 (above): Face-lift EPB sets operate on the Central and Eastern divisions, and are allocated to Selhurst and Slade Green depots. These sets can be immediately recognised from non face-lift stock as they are numbered above both cab windows. Set No. 5431 approaches Motspur Park, on 14th June 1983, whilst working the 08.42 Waterloo to Dorking service. The unit had been borrowed from the Central Division due to a shortage of stock.

Colin J. Marsden

Plate 50 (left): From 1982, the SR-designed 2EPB units have been passing through Eastleigh and Horwich works for a face-lift programme. This work included new upholstery, modern lighting, modern internal fittings and a public address system. Sets so treated are again numbered above both front windows. Unit No. 6301, formerly No. 5671, approaches Norwood Junction on 19th October 1981 with a Tattenham Corner to London Bridge working.

Colin J. Marsden

4CEP and 4BEP

CEP

Between the years of 1956-63, a total of 133 BEP/CEP units was introduced, basically for operation on the Kent Coast electrification scheme.

The CEP units were the first main line sets built to BR standard coach design, based on the Mk. 1 fleet of the period. Construction of CEP four coach units was carried out at Eastleigh and, by mid-1956, the first of four pre-production sets emerged as No. 7101. The unit had end corridor connections with a full gangway within the set. Technical equipment was similar to that used on BR-designed EPB stock. The formation of the four car units was: Motor Brake Second Open (MBSO), Trailer Composite Corridor (TCK), Trailer Second Corridor (TSK) and MBSO. MBSO vehicles contained the driver's compartment, with a guard's and luggage van behind, followed by passenger accommodation in an open layout. The two trailer vehicles were of similar construction, one housing three second and four first class compartments, and the other eight second class compartments, access to both vehicles being by a side corridor. Traction equipment for the fleet was two English Electric 250hp traction motors, mounted on the outer ends of each MBSO vehicle. The four prototype units operated on the Central Section and proved to be highly successful. A production fleet, given Nos. 7105-53, was ordered during 1957/8, and these were destined for phase 1 of the Kent Coast electrification scheme. They closely followed the prototype sets, but incorporated some modified technical equipment. A further fleet of units was ordered in 1960 for the second phase of the Kent Coast electrification scheme, and numbered 7154-7204. During 1962, a further seven units, Nos. 7205-7211, were ordered for the South Western Division, but these soon joined their brothers on the South Eastern Division.

BEP

To work with the CEP fleet, a batch of buffet units, classified BEP, was ordered. Two BEP units, Nos. 7001-2 worked with the four prototype CEP units. Construction was carried out alongside the CEP build at Eastleigh, and was identical, except for a TRB buffet vehicle, with 21 unclassified seats, replacing a TSK. Power for the buffet car was provided by its own motor generator mounted underneath. When the CEP production fleet was authorised, buffet sets were also ordered. Nos. 7003-7012 were for use with Nos. 7105-53, and Nos. 7013-22 for operation with Nos. 7154-7204.

The allocation of units remained constant for many years, with prototype sets Nos. 7001-2 and 7101-4 being used from Brighton Depot, and the production sets from Ramsgate. When delivered, units were painted in BR green livery which subsequently changed to rail blue, and later to Inter-City blue/grey.

With little possibility of new main line stock, a decision was taken to carry out a major refurbishing programme on the CEP/BEP fleet. Prior to large investment being made, set No. 7153 was experimentally refurbished at BREL Eastleigh. The work included alteration to the unit formation; the brake compartment was removed from the driving cars making these DMS (Driving Motor Second). The former trailer composite was rebuilt into a trailer brake composite, while the trailer second compartment was altered to an open carriage. After evaluation of No. 7153, a full refurbishing programme was authorised, and BREL Swindon was awarded the work. Transformation at Swindon commenced in 1979, with the final unit returning to the Southern Region in 1984. Quite early in the refurbishment programme it was decided that all buffet sets would not be required, and a number of BEP units were rebuilt to CEP standards, gaining a newly-converted locomotive-hauled TSO in place of the buffet car. It was decided to refurbish seven BEP units for use on the Portsmouth line, and these followed the CEP styling, with buffet cars being completely rebuilt providing a fast food facility.

Refurbished units were given the TOPS number system, CEP units emerging in the 411XXX fleet and BEP units in the 412XXX series.

In 1985, all CEP units were operating on the South Eastern Division and BEP units on the South Western. It should be noted that, as a 'stop-gap', four refurbished CEP units were temporarily remarshalled with unrefurbished BEP buffet cars in 1983-85 for Central Division operation, due to a shortage of buffet sets.

Plate 51 : Painted in distinctive all-over green livery with yellow numbering and lettering, 4CEP unit No. 7209 departs from Dorking North on 8th August 1964 with the 09.18 Victoria to Portmouth Harbour train. This unit was one of the final seven built for Western Section operation.

John Scrace

Plate 52 (left): The production CEP/BEP fleets have always been associated with the South Eastern Division, being allocated to Ramsgate Depot and operating the majority of South Eastern main line services. Set No. 7146, leading a BEP/CEP set, approaches Ashford on 15th May 1980 with a Victoria to Dover Western Docks train.

Colin J. Marsden

Plate 54 (right): The CEP/BEP refurbishing programme, which was undertaken by BREL Swindon, commenced in 1979 and continued until the spring of 1984. On completion, units were hauled back to the SR at Strawberry Hill where recommissioning took place. Occasionally, if Strawberry Hill was unable to accept the stock, it was outstabled at either Twickenham or Clapham Junction. Set No. 1555 is seen at Twickenham on 26th April 1983 where it was stored for some six weeks.

Colin J. Marsden

Plate 55 (below right): When refurbished CEP units (Class 411) returned to the SR, they were the first SR electric multiple units to carry six digit TOPS numbers. After only a short period, it was decided that the numbers were too long for daily recognition and that only the last four numbers would be used, the '41' prefix being omitted after only a handful of sets were completed. Set No. 411516 heads south near Paddock Wood on 4th June 1982 with a Victoria to Folkestone Harbour boat train.

Colin J. Marsden

Plate 53 (below): During the early 1980s while the CEP/BEP refurbishing programme was underway, a number of BEP units were put into Central Division operation. Some had their buffet cars isolated while others remained in use. Set No. 7017 passes Earlswood Junction heading a twelve car formation off the Redhill line, with a Victoria to Littlehampton train, on 28th April 1982.

Colin J. Marsden

2HAP, 2SAP and 4CAP

Two different builds of HAP stock have been constructed, some to SR Bulleid design and others to BR standard coach style.

The SR-designed units were constructed on reclaimed 2NOL underframes during 1956/8. Each two coach unit was formed of a Motor Brake Second Open (MBSO) and a Driving Trailer Composite (DTC), which also included a toilet. MBSO vehicles closely followed similar vehicles in EPB sets, and provided accommodation in the 3 + 2 configuration in open saloons. The DTC vehicle consisted of a second class coupé behind the driving position, with the rest of the coach having a side corridor feeding four second and three first class compartments, with a toilet housed at the inner end. When constructed, units were numbered 5601-36 and were intended for use on the Thanet routes, where they remained in operation until 1969 when some sets were transferred to the South Western Division for Waterloo to Windsor/Weybridge routes. Once on the South Western Division, units lost their first class accommodation and were reclassified as 2SAP. After a short period, the units were transferred to the 'Coastway' route when the first class accommodation was restored. In 1976, sets were again transferred back to the London Division, this time on the Central Section, for suburban work, and this once again meant the removal of first class accommodation. Stock remained in operation until the late 1970s when, in connection with the EPB facelift programme, it was decided to utilize the HAP (SAP) MBSO vehicles to form additional EPB units, using converted SUB vehicles as trailers, resulting in the withdrawal and scrapping of DTC vehicles.

About the same time as the above units were under construction, a larger fleet of BR-designed HAP units was built at Eastleigh Works. These resembled the BR-designed EPB units of the mid-1950s and were intended as replacements for HAL stock on the Gillingham and Maidstone routes. The first BR HAP unit, No. 6001, emerged in June 1957 in the MBSO, DTC formation. Passenger accommodation in the MBSO vehicle was basically the same as in the SR-designed sets but the DTC layout was revised. Three first class compartments were situated behind the driving cab, fed by a side corridor, and this was followed by two toilets and a five bay second class saloon. Each unit had a total seating capacity for 19 first and 134 second class passengers. Traction and control equipment was supplied by English Electric and the traction motors were fitted with express gear ratios.

The initial order was for 42 BR HAP units, but prior to the final units being delivered, subsequent orders were placed, firstly for 63 sets, Nos. 6043-6105, for use on the Thanet lines. For operation on the second phase of the Kent Coast electrification scheme a further fleet, numbered 6106-46, was ordered. The final batch of HAP units came in 1962/3 when units Nos. 6147-73 were built for South Western and Central operation.

The BR HAP fleet remained intact until 1973 when, due to a severe shortage of suburban stock, some South Western Division-allocated sets were downgraded to second class only, reclassified as 2SAP and renumbered in the 59XX series. By 1979/80, the stock position had changed and these units then returned to their HAP status. During 1982, a further reshuffle of SR stock resulted in 46 sets being semi-permanently coupled in pairs for use on the 'Coastway' line. Units so treated were reclassified 4CAP ('Coastway' HAP) and renumbered in the 32XX and 33XX series. These sets remained on the 'Coastway' route between Ore and Portsmouth until May 1984 when they were reallocated to Ramsgate.

Due to a large number of HAP units having blue asbestos, withdrawal commenced in late 1982, and it is expected that the majority will have been withdrawn by mid-1986. Ten withdrawn HAP MBSO vehicles were completely rebuilt, in 1983/4 at BREL Eastleigh, into Gatwick luggage vans (GLV) for the new 'Gatwick Express' service.

When introduced, HAP units were finished in BR green livery, but were subsequently changed to BR blue and, in more recent years, to blue/grey colours.

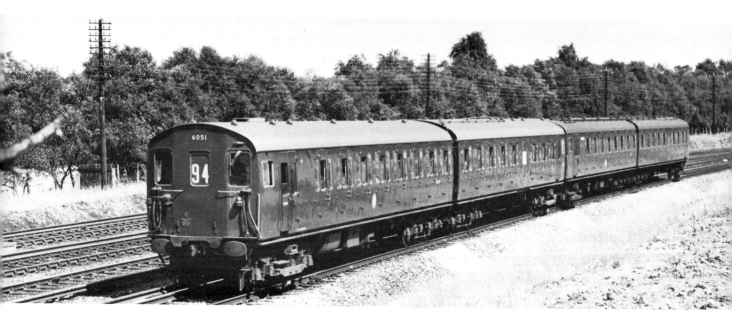

Plate 56 (above): The BR 2HAP units were designed primarily for operation on the South Eastern Section. Within the build, a number of detail differences exist depending on the period of manufacture. A four car HAP formation, led by unit No. 6051, approaches Chislehurst on 30th June 1959 with a Charing Cross to Kent Coast working.

Colin J. Marsden

Plate 57 (left): The SR Bulleid-designed HAP units numbered in the 56XX range were very similiar to the two car EPB sets, and indeed, in later years, most MBSO coaches were used for forming additional 4EPB units. 2HAP unit No. 5630, with its MBSO nearest the camera, stands at Ashford, Kent, on 25th August 1964, whilst station rebuilding work was being carried out. Note the destination board on the unit side.

Alec Swain

Plate 58 (above): By the early 1960s, the BR-designed HAP fleet had settled down on the Eastern Section and often operated in ten car formations. The reliability level of this stock was high, and during 1962 a 93 per cent availability was recorded. No. 6055 leads four other HAP units through Bellingham on 10th September 1960 with the 13.28 Victoria to Ramsgate service.

John Scrace

Plate 59 (below): Due to reallocation of the SR-designed HAP stock, on more than one occasion the first class accommodation was downgraded, thus reclassifying the units as 2SAP. During the late 1970s and early 1980s, when the stock operated from Selhurst Depot on Central suburban duties, all first class seating was removed and the stock operated alongside the EPB fleet. No. 5610 passes through the Selhurst washing machine on 5th March 1982.

Colin J. Marsden

Plate 60 (above): Over the years, reallocation has also meant that the BR HAP fleet has operated on all three divisions. The South Eastern Division, who once had the majority of sets, were left with just five by the summer of 1984, and none by 1985. On 5th February 1981, South Western Division-allocated No. 6015 leads a semi-fast Waterloo to Basingstoke/Alton train near West Byfleet.

Colin J. Marsden

Plate 61 (left): In the early 1980s, a number of Ramsgate-allocated HAP units were reallocated to Wimbledon, as the operating department wished to eliminate non-corridor stock from the South Eastern Division at the earliest opportunity. HAP unit No. 6095, with a 4VEP at the rear, approaches Wimbledon on 11th January 1982 whilst working the 08.16 Waterloo (Windsor) to Waterloo (Main) service.

Colin J. Marsden

Plate 62 (above): Since their introduction, a number of alterations have been made to HAP stock with down grading, etc. However, one of the most curious alterations came in 1982 when forty six sets were semi-permanently coupled in pairs to operate on the 'Coastway' service; units so treated being reclassified as 4CAP and renumbered. 4CAP set No. 3206 approaches Eastbourne on 4th August 1982 with the 16.42 Ore to Brighton train.

Colin J. Marsden

Plate 63 (right): Although the CAP units were specially formed to operate on the 'Coastway' route, the stock was reallocated to the South Eastern Division at Ramsgate from May 1984 for main line operation, thus returning non-corridor stock to the South Eastern Division. 4CAP set No. 3311 departs slowly from Fratton, on 12th June 1982, with the 17.32 Brighton to Portsmouth Harbour train.

Colin J. Marsden

MLV and TLV

After the introduction of the Kent Coast electrification scheme, the Southern were keen to use electric multiple unit formations on London to Dover boat trains, but if CEP/BEP stock was used, luggage accommodation would be limited. It was therefore decided to construct two single coach motor luggage vans (MLV), which were basically motorised BG vehicles with driving controls at both ends. Each van had two luggage compartments with a small guard's position. Traction equipment consisted of two 275hp traction motors, and the vehicles were compatible to all post-1951 built electric multiple units except Class 455. A special fitting on MLVs enabled them to operate off the electrified area, gaining power for traction from on-board traction batteries. This proved especially useful if vehicles were required to operate to loading points at docks or quays which were not electrified.

In addition to traction batteries, a vacuum exhauster was provided enabling the cars to haul a 100 ton trailing load of vacuum-fitted stock. The two MLVs were numbered 68001-2, and emerged in 1958. When the second phase of the Kent Coast electrification scheme was underway, which would include the lines to Folkestone, a further 8 MLVs were con-structed to the same design, and numbered 68003-10. The MLV fleet is still much in evidence today and can regularly be seen marshalled, usually at the London end of boat trains.

By the summer of 1963, it was found that such was the luggage loadings on boat trains that only one van was insufficient, and so to overcome this problem a number of trains operated with two luggage vans. As there were only ten luggage vans, when doubling up was required an acute shortage of these vehicles occurred. This resulted in the introduction of six trailer luggage vans (TLV), Nos. 68201-6, during 1968. These were conventional BG vehicles, wired for electric multiple unit operation and fitted with EP brake equipment. The corridor ends were retained but sealed out of use, conversion work being carried out at Selhurst.

Following the general decline in the transportation of luggage on dock routes, the TLVs were taken out of service in 1975 and stored. They later saw use as match wagons for the transferring of new REP/TC trailer vehicles from York Works to the Southern Region, and are now used in departmental stock as 'en-part' vehicles, carrying locomotive parts, between the Western Region and Doncaster Works.

Plate 64 (below): The entire fleet of motor luggage vans (MLV), or Class 419 stock, is allocated to Ramsgate, and usually operate on the London end of Folkestone/Dover to London boat trains. No. 68006 storms through Paddock Wood on 23rd June 1983 with a Dover to Victoria boat train. When first introduced, the MLV stock only carried their numbers on the coach sides, but in recent years the numbers have been applied to the front ends.

Colin J. Marsden

4CIG and 4BIG

By the early 1960s, new stock was projected for SR main line operation, as most of the present main line units were nearing retiring age. During 1962/3, plans were drawn up for a new generation of electric multiple units, based on the external design of the CEP units. However, it was decided to have a break from the previous SR tradition. The driving vehicles were no longer to carry traction equipment or the guard's compartment, and all power and control equipment was to be housed in a Motor Brake Second (MBS), formed in the middle of a four car set. During 1962, orders were placed for Brighton line replacement stock, which consisted of thirty six 4CIG (four car Corridor Intermediate Guards) and nineteen 4BIG (four car Buffet Intermediate Guards) units. Formations were: CIG — Driving Trailer Composite (DTC), Motor Brake Second (MBS), Trailer Second (TS), DTC; BIG — these were the same as CIG units except for the TS car being replaced by a Trailer Buffet (TRB). Another break from previous was that the build was carried out at York, who had a long history of electric multiple unit and coach building.

Each unit incorporated two DTC vehicles of slightly different layout. One was set out with three first and one second class compartments, a three bay second class saloon with toilets at the inner end; the other vehicle had four first class compartments, a three bay second class saloon and two toilets. The MBS vehicles were mounted on two motor bogies, each axle having a 250hp traction motor, control equipment being mounted between the bogies. The internal layout consisted of a small luggage cage, guard's office and 6½ second class seating bays. TS cars were basically a Mk. I locomotive-hauled TSO having accommodation for 72 in nine bays of eight. In BIG units, the buffet car provided accom-

modation for 40 second class passengers. The appearance of sets was similar to CEP/BRP builds, but incorporated a number of detail alterations, including a modified end gangway and the recessing of end pipe/control cables under the driver's windows. The first CIG unit, No. 7301, was constructed by York in 1963/4 and delivered in the autumn of 1964; the final unit of the initial build being delivered in early 1966. The BIG fleet, numbered 7031-48, was not delivered until late 1965.

In the closing years of the 1960s, new stock was envisaged for the Waterloo to Portsmouth route and a further order for fleets of CIG/BIG units was placed. These were of the same internal layout as previous builds, except for a more modern decor, together with some technical refinements. Unit numbers for Portsmouth line stock were 7337-66 for CIG units, and 7049-58 for BIG units. In 1969, a further order for 71 CIG units was placed and allocated numbers 7367-7437, delivery commencing in 1970 with allocation to the South Western and Central divisions to replace COR and other ageing stock. Before the end of the CIG production run, one further unit, No. 7438, was ordered as a replacement for a withdrawn CEP unit.

The CIG/BIG fleets gradually took over London to South Coast duties which were previously operated by COR/BUF/GRI/PAN and PUL stock, on both the Central and South Western divisions, being allocated to Brighton and Fratton depots. Under the TOPS system, CIG units were classified as 421 and BIG units 420. The original units for the Brighton line were outshopped in green, whereas later units emerged painted in Inter-City blue/grey livery.

Plate 65 (above): Today it looks quite strange to see 1963-designed stock in anything but blue/grey livery. However, when the original fleets of CIG and BIG units entered service they carried multiple unit green livery. A BIG/CIG formation, led by BIG unit No. 7046, is illustrated here in green livery, as seen in September 1966.

British Rail

Plate 66 (above): When introduced, the BIG fleet was divided between Brighton and Fratton depots, operating Victoria and Waterloo services respectively. From mid-1983, the Fratton allocation was transferred to Brighton and replaced by refurbished Class 410 (412) stock. 4BIG unit No. 7038 emerges from the Quarry line at Coulsdon North on 19th October 1982 with a Brighton to London Bridge semi-fast service.

Colin J. Marsden

Plate 67 (below): The 138-strong 4CIG fleet is allocated to the Central and South Western divisions, with Brighton and Fratton depots being responsible for their maintenance. 4CIG unit No. 7336 overtakes a 4VEP between Gloucester Road Junction and East Croydon on 19th October 1982 with a London Bridge to Brighton duty.

Colin J. Marsden

3TC, 4TC and 4REP

The Waterloo to Bournemouth line was electrified west of Pirbright Junction during 1965-7. The Southern Region, who still wanted to operate a through passenger service between London and Weymouth, were faced with the problem that if electric multiple unit stock was used, it would be necessary for it to be locomotive-operated beyond Bournemouth, but this would be both uneconomic and operationally undesirable. To overcome this difficulty, an elaborate push-pull system was developed, using one high power 'tractor' unit, classified as 4REP, which could propel/haul four or eight TC (Trailer Control) cars between Waterloo and Bournemouth, from where the TC sets were hauled by a modified Class 33 locomotive on to Weymouth, discarding the tractor set at Bournemouth. The Class 33s were specially modified for these duties and could be controlled from the remote cab of the TC set by means of 27 wire control jumpers and a westcode system.

The 4REP (four car Restaurant Electro-Pneumatic) sets were constructed at York Works and were formed of a Driving Motor Second (DMS), Trailer Restaurant Buffet (TRB), Trailer Brake First (TBF) and DMS. Each DMS had a standard driving cab at the outer end with a transverse walkway behind; passenger accommodation being provided in two four bay saloons separated by a central vestibule. The power equipment, housed under the coach, consisted of 4 x 400hp English Electric traction motors, one mounted on each axle. The two trailer vehicles were rebuilds from former locomotive-hauled Mk. I coaches, modernisation being undertaken at York Works. The TRB cars were rebuilds from 1961 vintage RB vehicles, with very little alteration to the seating area, but the cooking facilities were completely rebuilt. TBF vehicles were again rebuilt from Mk. I stock, this time CK vehicles, and major alterations included the removal of the second class compartments and the constructing of a guard's office and security compartment. The first class accommodation was also modified to the latest standard. To cover the advertised passenger services, a fleet of eleven REP units was introduced, but no provision for expansion of the service was allowed for and, by 1974, four additional REP units were required, and were again constructed at York Works. DMS vehicles were identical to the previous type, the TRB/TBF cars again being rebuilds. TBF vehicles followed the previous styling but TRB cars were rebuilt from redundant RU vehicles and had a number of detail differences.

The initial fleet was numbered 3001-11 and was painted in standard rail blue, but this subsequently changed to blue/grey from the early 1970s. The 1974-built sets, Nos. 3012-15, emerged in blue/grey from new.

To operate with REP units, a fleet of three and four car TC sets was introduced and these were all rebuilds of Mk. I locomotive-hauled vehicles. The 3TC units, Nos. 301-303, later augmented into four car units, were formed as follows: Driving Trailer Second (DTS), Trailer Brake Second (TBS), DTS, whilst the four car sets, Nos. 401-428, were formed of a DTS, TBS, Trailer First Corridor (TFK) and a DTS. The TC units' DTS vehicles were rebuilt from Mk. I TSO coaches, the position of the two former toilets being rebuilt into a driving cab and adjoining vestibule. TBS cars were modified from Mk. I BSK vehicles, the internal layout remaining basically the same with just the decor modernised. TFK coaches were rebuilds of Mk. I FK stock, updated to conform to modern standards. The formation of three 3TC sets primarily came about because if two 4TC and one 3TC were coupled together, and hauled by a locomotive, they would occupy the same platform space as a twelve car electric multiple unit formation. They were also envisaged for possible use on the rear of service trains to convey passengers to Southampton Docks, being 'tripped' into the docks from Southampton Station. When the additional REP units were introduced in 1974/5, some additional 4TC sets were also built. The three car formations were augmented to four car by the addition of a TFK and three 'new' sets came into service. All vehicles were again converted from locomotive-hauled stock at York Works and numbered 429-434.

Plate 68 (below): Although the electric multiple unit operating principle was established on the SR many years ago, and the majority of staff were trained in its operation, when the REP/TC 'tractor and trailer' system was introduced during the mid-1960s for the Waterloo – Bournemouth – Weymouth route, a major training programme had again to be undertaken. A 4TC and 4REP formation approaches New Malden on 3rd March 1967 with a testing and training special, bound for Basingstoke.

Colin J. Marsden Collection

Plate 69 (above): It is usual operating practice for the REP units to be coupled at the London end of formations, thus facilitating the rapid removal of the TC stock at Bournemouth, and the efficient loading of the buffet car at Waterloo. 4REP unit No. 3002 arrives at Eastleigh in August 1968 with a semi-fast Bournemouth to Waterloo train.

Colin Boocock

Plate 70 (below): Today, REP/TC formations operate an hourly fast and an hourly semi-fast service between Waterloo and Bournemouth, the fast train having the TC portion taken forward to Weymouth. A semi-fast Bournemouth to Waterloo train passes Hampton Court Junction on 4th April 1980 led by REP unit No. 3003.

Colin J. Marsden

Plate 71 (right): The REP units with their 3,300 available hp are the most powerful electric multiple unit stock in daily operation, but when the additional weight of the TC stock is taken into account, the available power/weight is not much in excess of a 12VEP/CIG formation. REP unit No. 3012 leads two 4TC sets round the tight curve approaching Millbrook on 7th April 1983, with the 08.34 Weymouth to Waterloo service.

Colin J. Marsden

Plate 72 (below): With the REP traction unit on the rear being controlled via the 27 wire control jumpers, the 10.45 Waterloo to Bournemouth brakes for the Winchester stop on 19th August 1983 as it passes the Baltic Siding with TC set No. 402 leading. The semi-fast services from Waterloo to Bournemouth have nine intermediate stops on the 108 mile journey, with an average time of 2hr. 6min.

Colin J. Marsden

Plate 73 (above): The fast services from Waterloo to Bournemouth and Weymouth run non-stop to Southampton, and then go forward to Bournemouth, covering the 108 miles in 1hr. 38min. Storming through the New Forest near Beaulieu Road, on 7th April 1983, is the 10.35 Waterloo to Weymouth working with TC set No. 421 providing the leading driving position.

Colin J. Marsden

Plate 74 (below): All REP/TC stock is allocated to Bournemouth depot where routine maintenance is carried out. However, the units regularly travel to Chart Leacon Depot at Ashford (Kent) where bogie overhauls are undertaken. REP unit No. 3003 provides the traction power for the 13.00 Bournemouth to Waterloo train on 3rd August 1983 and is seen heading through the Hampshire countryside, near Fleet.

Colin J. Marsden

Plate 75 (above): When the TC stock originally entered service during 1966/7 it was confined to use on the Bournemouth/Weymouth line. However, in recent years, their operation range has widened and the stock, obtaining its power from a Class 33/1 locomotive, now works daily on the Waterloo to Salisbury, Clapham Junction to Kensington Olympia lines, in addition to weekend workings on the Reading to Portsmouth route. Class 33/1 locomotive No. 33113 heads TC set No. 409 near Oakley with the 08.34 Basingstoke to Salisbury train on 7th July 1981.

Colin J. Marsden

Plate 76 (right): When coupled to either a REP unit or a Class 33 locomotive, the TC stock would be unable to obtain sufficient air for its needs from the traction unit compressors, therefore each TC set is fitted with a compressor, mounted under the brake vehicle. TC set No. 404 leads another of the class, and a Class 33/1 locomotive, towards Worting Junction on 7th July 1981 with the 07.55 Salisbury to Waterloo service.

Colin J. Marsden

4VEC and 3TIS

Perhaps the most unusual of the SR electrified lines is the Isle of Wight system. In 1965, the line and its ancient equipment was due for retirement and a strong rumour was that the Island railway would be closed, and this was substantiated when the Beeching axe fell on the entire Island network. Following the enormous public outcry against this proposal, it was eventually decided to keep open the most heavily used section between Ryde and Shanklin. The BR Board was then faced with the problem of stock replacement as the restricted loading gauge precluded the use of mainland vehicles. About this time, it was found that London Transport (LT) had a surplus of 1920-30 built tube stock. BR was interested, and subsequently purchased about 55 cars, although only 42 actually went to the Island, the remainder being scrapped. Initially, it was the intention to convert these cars to diesel operation using Gardner bus engines, but it was subsequently decided that operation would be more effective if the system was electrified.

The Island electrification scheme commenced in January 1966 and was completed in 15 months. Prior to the LT stock being transferred to BR, it was technically overhauled at Acton Works and then moved to Stewarts Lane for completion, and formed into sets of six three car and six four car units, enabling seven car train formations. Three car units were classified as TIS and formed of Motor Brake Second Open (MBSO), Trailer Second Open (TSO) and Driving Trailer Second Open (DTSO), while four car sets, classified VEC, were formed of MBSO, TSO, DTSO (non-operational) and MBSO. The SR codes VEC-TIS are derived from the Roman name for the Isle of Wight — Vectis. The MBSO cars have a small equipment compartment behind the driving cab containing all technical and control equipment, and two 240hp MV traction motors on each MBSO. Total seating on TIS sets is 106 and VEC units 132, with sufficient standing room for an equal number. After sets were formed at Stewarts Lane, testing and training took place on the London to Woking section of the South Western Division, prior to the cars being assembled at Fratton for removal by low loaders to the Island.

The passenger services on the Island commenced from 20th March 1967, and the stock has remained in service ever since, receiving all maintenance at Ryde St. John's Depot. When introduced, the stock was painted in rail blue livery with full yellow warning ends. This remained until the late 1970s when some sets emerged from Ryde Depot with grey doors. In 1982, when no new stock for the Island was foreseen, a light refurbishing programme on the ageing stock was chosen. Units so treated emerged painted in Inter-City blue/grey and were adorned with their six figure TOPS number, set numbers allocated to three car sets being 031-036 and four car units 041-046; TOPS classification being 486 and 485 respectively. It is unusual for trains to operate in seven coach formation, but four car sets have been known, especially on the Ryde Pier Head to Ryde Esplanade shuttle. It is still uncertin when, if ever, new stock will be provided for the Island, and the present units now hold the distinction of being the oldest electric stock operating in Britain.

Plate 78 (above): Today, the Isle of Wight railway is something of a living museum, being totally isolated from the mainland system. Depot and small works facilities exist at Ryde where any repairs from changing a lamp to body repairs can be undertaken. Approaching Ryde St. John's Road, refurbished set No. 486036 forms the 18.11 Shanklin to Ryde Pier Head service on 14th June 1982.

Colin J. Marsden

Plate 79 (left): The six three car and six four car units which usually operate in seven car formations, provide the entire rail passenger service on the Island, and during the summer months a basic 20 minute service is operated from 07.00 until 23.00. Departing from Sandown and heading for Brading, 4VEC and 3TIS units Nos. 044 and 034 form the 10.41 Shanklin to Ryde service on 14th June 1982.

Colin J. Marsden

Plate 80 (right): This ex-London Transport tube stock, which is now over fifty years old, must soon be up for replacement. Regretfully, due to limited clearances on the Island, conventional stock cannot be used, and finding replacement stock will be difficult. A seven car formation departs from Brading during the summer of 1982 with the 12.30 Ryde Pier Head to Shanklin train.

Colin J. Marsden

Plate 77 (left): After a decision was made to use redundant LT tube stock on the 'new' Isle of Wight railway, and rebuilding work had been completed, there was the major job of moving the vehicles from the mainland to the island. All cars were taken by rail to Fratton from where they were mounted on the back of Pickford low loaders, and transported via the Fishbourne car ferry. This view, photographed on 2nd September 1966, shows the first coach to be delivered being taken through the streets of Ryde, whilst en route to St. John's Road Depot.

British Rail

4VEP, 4VEG and 8VAB

With the electrification of the Bournemouth route in 1967, new main line/outer suburban stock was required, and orders were therefore placed for a fleet of twenty high density units similar to the successful CIG design of a few years earlier. These units were given the designation 4VEP — four coach Vestibule Electro-Pneumatic; the main difference between CIG and VEP stock being the number of passenger seats available. In CIG units, the seats were arranged in the 2 + 2 low density mode, with only a few access doors on each coach, whereas on VEP stock, seating was provided in the 3 + 2 high density style with doors by each seating bay. The formation of VEP stock is Driving Trailer Composite (DTC), Motor Brake Second (MBS), Trailer Second Open (TSO) and DTC. The DTC vehicle has a normal driving cab with a transverse walkway behind, a four bay saloon and a four compartment first class section accessible by a side corridor. The MBS vehicle, which houses all power and control equipment, is set out as a six bay saloon, the remainder housing a guard's office and luggage cage. TSO vehicles are arranged in ten bays, with the end ones accommodating eight passengers and the remainder ten.

The main power equipment for the VEP build was supplied by English Electric (GEC) in the form of 4 x 250hp traction motors. The initial order was placed in 1965 for twenty sets, numbered 7701-20, and before delivery of the last one of this batch, a subsequent order for 95 was placed. These were for the Central Division and numbered 7721-7815 and, again, before this order had been completed, yet a further 38 units were ordered and received the numbers 7816-53. These were to replace HAL/COR units on the South Western and Central divisions. In 1973, the final contract for VEP units was placed when unit Nos. 7854-7894 were ordered for the South Eastern Division, to replace HAP stock on main line duties. Construction of all but the TSO and MBS vehicles of the first twenty units

was carried out by the railway workshops at York, the TSO and MBS cars of Nos. 7701-20 being constructed at Derby (Litchurch Lane). Early units were outshopped in all blue livery which subsequently changed to blue/grey. Units constructed after 1971 were painted in Inter-City colours from new.

When units Nos. 7739/41/42 were delivered in 1968, they were disbanded and the vehicles were used to form a special eight coach unit coded VAB, No. 8001. This set, made up of a five and three car unit, containing three power cars, was intended for use on the Bournemouth line when shortage of REP stock prevailed. The three car portion was formed of a DTC, MBS and a DTC, and the five car section, a DTC, MBS, TRB (Trailer Restaurant Buffet), MBS and a DTC; the TRB being locomotive-hauled buffet No. S1759, which was wired for multiple unit operation. The VAB was only in use when other stock was unavailable, and after the delivery of the four additional REP units in 1974, was disbanded with most cars reverting back into VEP stock.

Apart from the formation of the VAB, the VEP fleet remained intact until 1978 when twelve units, Nos. 7788-99, were reclassified as VEG (Vestibule Electro-Gatwick), and the interiors were altered to provide extra luggage accommodation for Victoria to Gatwick passengers. Externally, units were identified by the 'Rail-Air' slogan, which was applied on the body side and at cant rail height. When reclassified as VEG units they were renumbered 7901-12. From May 1984, the twelve VEG sets were returned to their VEP state following the introduction of the 'Gatwick Express' service.

In 1984, the VEP fleet was allocated to all three divisions and was responsible for some 75 per cent of outer suburban duties. The fleet is expected to remain in service well into the next century.

Plate 82 (right): The VEP fleet is allocated to all three Southern divisions, and is used on a number of inner and outer suburban duties. South Western Division-allocated No. 7824 departs from Swaythling on 7th July 1981 with the 14.42 Waterloo to Bournemouth slow service.

Colin J. Marsden

Plate 81 (below left): Painted in its distinctive all-over blue livery with full yellow warning end, No. 7743 passes Haywards Heath, on 1st June 1968, with the 10.12 London Bridge to Brighton service. When introduced, the VEP units had orange curtains in both first and second class areas, but today those in the second class portions have been removed.

John Scrace

Plate 83 (below): The passenger environment within VEP stock is good with comfortable seating, plenty of light, good ventilation and easy toilet access. VEP unit No. 7814, leading a 4EPB unit, passes Barnes with the 13.05 Reading to Waterloo train on 27th October 1982.

Colin J. Marsden

Plate 84 (above): South Western Division VEP units are allocated to Wimbledon, Bournemouth and Fratton depots and share operations with CIG stock on main line duties. On a sunny 11th May 1980, two VEP units, led by No. 7704, pass Weybridge with the 16.46 Waterloo to Bournemouth service, deputising for a failed REP/TC formation.

Colin J. Marsden

Plate 85 (left): One of the largest Southern Region servicing depots is Wimbledon East, which has around 150 electric multiple unit sets on its books. With the depot in the background housing VEP, 508 and SUB stock, 4VEP unit No. 7818 provides the leading unit on the 11.00 (Sundays) Waterloo to Basingstoke service during October 1982.

Colin J. Marsden

Plate 86 (right): To provide additional luggage space for passengers travelling between Victoria and Gatwick, twelve VEP sets were modified with altered seating, during the late 1970s, and were in use until the 'Gatwick Express' service was introduced from May 1984. The altered sets were classified VEG, and renumbered. VEG unit No. 7903 emerges from the picturesque Clayton Tunnel, near Brighton, on 28th April 1982 with a fast Brighton to Victoria service.

Colin J. Marsden

Plate 87 (below): One of the most unique electric multiple units to operate has been the VAB set, formed of VEP coaches together with a locomotive-hauled buffet car. The unit was introduced in 1967, due to a shortage of buffet-equipped stock on the Bournemouth line, and remained in service until the mid-1970s when additional REP units were introduced. The unit was always recognisable as the VEP cars were in rail blue livery, while the buffet car was in Inter-City colours. The unit is seen here near Southampton in August 1968.

Colin Boocock

2PEP and 4PEP

The first plans for 'new' generation electric multiple unit stock were put forward during the late 1960s, as many of the current types would be scheduled for replacement in the foreseeable future. In 1970, a decision was made to construct a prototype electric multiple unit, which would incorporate a number of basic changes from previous tradition, to operate on the Southern Region. Two four coach and one two coach unit were eventually built and the design was a total change. Sliding doors, and low-backed 2 + 2 seating, with a sloping body profile at the bottom, were provided for passengers. Front end design also differed from previous practice, and no side buffers were provided, all end stresses being transmitted through a central coupling which also included air and electrical connections. Passenger accommodation was in open layout coaches with seats in the 2 + 2 configuration with large gangways, providing 68 seats in driving cars and 72 seats in intermediate vehicles. Passenger access was by double-leaf sliding doors, two pairs each side on driving cars and three on intermediate vehicles, and although doors were under the supervisory control of the guard, they could be opened by passengers. Another break from previous SR practice was for all the vehiles to be powered, thus providing a high acceleration rate; a basic requirement for a modern reliable railway. Braking was provided by the standard EP system, as well as a rheostatic unit which used current generated during acceleration for speed retardation.

The first 'new' generation evaluation set, classified by the Southern Region as PEP, was four car unit No. 4001, which arrived on the Southern Region in May 1971. By the end of the year, it was joined by sister set No. 4002, and commenced an intensive series of test runs, firstly on the Alton line and later in passenger service on the Waterloo to Shepperton, Hampton Court and Chessington routes. During 1972, the two coach set, No. 2001, emerged and, rather surprisingly, was left in unpainted aluminium. After testing, this set of vehicles took up trial running together with the four car units. In 1972, a reformation of vehicles took place and one of the unpainted aluminium cars found its way into a four car set. By 1974, the two car set, now sporting one blue and one aluminium coach, was transferred to the Railway Technical Centre (RTC) at Derby, where an additional unpowered trailer, fitted with a pantograph, was constructed for test running on both the Eastern and Scottish Regions, to pave the way for the eventual introduction of Class 313 and 314 sets. The two four car units continued to operate on the South Western Division until October 1976 when both went out of service and were stored. No. 4001 eventually went to Derby where it is still stored. No. 4002 also went to Derby for experimental bogie fittings, and returned to the Southern Region painted in an executive livery, and with traction equipment fitted to the outer ends of the driving cars only; the unit is now stored at Clapham Junction awaiting a decision on its future. A great deal of information was gained from the operation of these test units which eventually paved the way for the Class 313, 314, 315, 317, 455, 507 and 508 fleets.

Plate 88 (below): The first 'new generation' BR standard design electric multiple unit stock emerged in 1971 in the shape of three prototype passenger-carrying sets. A four car unit, No. 4002, is seen outside the shed at Wimbledon Park in 1973 while test running was carried out. A significant feature of this stock was that each wheel set was powered, giving a high acceleration rate.

British Rail

Plate 89 (above): A photograph of the original mock-up for 'new generation' electric multiple unit stock, produced by the design panel at Derby. As can be seen, the prototype stock closely followed this dummy except for a conventional 2-position headcode fitted in the central door window position.

British Rail

Plate 91 (right): Whilst the 'new generation' of suburban unit was under design it was decided to include many new and novel features previously unused by BR. These included fully automatic couplers of the 'Scharfenberg' type which incorporated physical, air and electrical connections. Two PEP front ends are seen coupled in this illustration.

Colin J. Marsden

Plate 90 (below): Another major advancement on 'new generation' electric multiple unit stock, classified as PEP by the SR, were sliding passenger-operated doors, facilitating rapid loading/unloading of the train. This illustration, dated by the style of dress, shows the door/window layout of an intermediate coach.

British Rail

1940 Waterloo & City Stock

By 1938, the Waterloo & City line had been in operation for forty years and the Southern Railway decided to refurbish the line and introduce new stock. English Electric at Preston were awarded a contract to construct twelve double-ended motor cars and sixteen trailers. These new vehicles, each measuring 47ft. in length, were fitted with air-operated sliding doors. Passenger accommodation was for 40 in motor cars and 52 in trailers, and large gangways were provided enabling a considerable number of standing passengers to be transported.

All traction and control equipment was supplied by English Electric and was mounted at one end of each motor car (the Bank end); each motor car being powered by two 190hp traction motors.

The formation of trains is usually five coaches (a motor coach at each end with three trailers between) however, during off-peak periods, two motor coaches may be coupled together to operate as a power twin. Technically, a single motor coach could operate on its own, but due to operating restrictions this is not permitted.

To operate a full service, four five car sets are required, and these are identified by letters carried on the nose end of sets. All regular maintenance is carried out in sidings at the Waterloo end of the line, with heavy and classified overhauls being dealt with at Selhurst.

One non-standard feature of the stock is that it carries red marker lights at both the front and rear when in service. Numbering of motor cars is S51-62 and trailers S71-86. When built, livery applied was SR green with silver ends, but today the livery is BR rail blue with grey ends. Some vehicles of this 1940 built stock were taken out of service during 1982/3 and stored, pending further refurbishment.

Plate 92 (below): Another isolated section of the SR is the Waterloo & City Railway, connecting Waterloo with Bank Station in the City of London. This purpose-built stock, introduced in 1940, is still in regular daily operation and is expected to be so for many years to come. A two car train, formed of two power cars, stands at Waterloo in August 1981.

Colin J. Marsden

Class 455

Southern Region purpose-designed and built suburban replacement stock was authorised in 1980, when a fleet of 74 four coach units was ordered and classified 510; this subsequently changed to Class 455. The 'new' generation stock, based on the Mk. III locomotive-hauled profile, followed the London Midland Region's Class 317 units off the York production line, and commenced delivery to the SR at the end of 1982. The Class 455 units reverted to the SR unit policy of the early 1960s by having the powered vehicle in the middle of the formation, but it did not incorporate guard's accommodation. Unit formations are: Driving Trailer Second (DTS), Motor Second (MS), Trailer Second (TS) and DTS. Passenger accommodation (all second class) is provided for 74 in DTS and 84 in intermediate vehicles, all laid out in the high density 2 + 3 configuration. Coach construction resembled the Class 508 build, but incorporated a revised front end, with a centre gangway and waist height control jumpers. Main reservoir pipes were also fitted in place of automatic connections under the tightlock coupling, used on the Class 508. Although the dynamic or rheostatic brake was fitted to the Class 508 units, and proved satisfactory, it could not be used on the Class 455, so conventional EP braking was used. Despite units having end control jumpers, they are incompatible with any other stock on BR and are, therefore, restricted to multiple operation within their own class. Construction of the first Class 455 unit commenced late in 1981 at BREL York, but was not completed until the late summer of 1982 when several finished units were transferred to BREL Wolverton Works for detail modifications. Actual delivery to the SR commenced from December 1982, and the 74 units had all been received on the region by April 1984. All the initial order was placed into South Western Division operation, firstly taking over on suburban duties and, later, on the Windsor/Weybridge services, and from May 1984 on the new Guildford line.

Upon delivery, units went to Strawberry Hill CM&EE Depot, near Twickenham, where all commissioning work was carried out. Unit numbers allocated were 455801-74, but as the SR only recognise units by the last four digits of six figure TOPS numbers, only the last four are actually applied to units.

In May 1984, the first of the second production run of 43 Class 455 units, No. 455701, was delivered, having a revised front end with air horns positioned under the buffer beam, and incorporating a Trailer Second (TS) from a Class 508. The third and probably final Class 455 — 455/9 — commenced production in early 1985 for twenty units, of which at least 5 are to be fitted with Thyristor chopper power equipment.

From spring 1985, the Class 455 commenced operation on the Central Division suburban services.

At the present time, the Class 455 units are operated by both a driver and guard, but units are wired for driver only operation, and it is the BR Board's intention to introduce this method of operation at an early opportunity.

Plate 93 (below): The first batch of 74 Class 455 units commenced delivery to SR at the end of 1982, and all had been received by July 1984, allocation of the entire fleet being to East Wimbledon. The stock is operated on all suburban diagrams replacing the majority of EPB types. Set No. 5818 passes the now closed Wimbledon West Yard on 26th May 1983 with the 13.34 Waterloo to Shepperton service.

Colin J. Marsden

Classes 488 and 489 'Gatwick Express'

For some years, the BR Board has been aware of the need for a rapid, frequent and reliable service between Gatwick Airport and London, Victoria Station. During the 1970s, as a stop-gap measure, a fleet of twelve VEP units was altered internally to accommodate passenger luggage on this rail-air link.

In the early 1980s, financial assistance was sought and granted for a new service, which culminated in the introduction of the 'Gatwick Express' service from 14th May 1984. Stock for this route is not new but has been adapted for its new duties, passenger accommodation being provided in rebuilt Mk. IIf coaches, coupled in semi-permanent two and three coach formations, classified as 488/2 and 488/3; each train being formed of two 488/3 three car sets and one 488/2 two coach set. The 488/2 sets are rebuilds of Mk. IIf FO and TSO cars bar-coupled together, with high level air and multiple control jumpers mounted on the set ends. The FO car, reclassified as Trailer First Handbrake (TFH), accommodates 41 passengers and has a toilet, additional luggage space being provided in the former second toilet position; a handbrake system has also been fitted. The second class coach, formerly a TSO, is now classified as Trailer Second Handbrake (TSH) and can seat 56 passengers with revised luggage accommodation as in TFH cars; handbrake equipment has again

been supplied. The three car sets, classified 488/3, are formed of three converted TSO vehicles, the two outer cars being the same as TSH vehicles in the Class 488/2 sets, with a TSO in the centre which is bar-coupled to both outer vehicles. The total passenger accommodation for a train formed of one Class 488/2 and two 488/3 sets is 433. All vehicles have been renumbered in the SR electric multiple unit range and allocated numbers 8201-8210 (488/2), and 8301-8319 (488/3).

Power for the 'Gatwick Express' is provided by Class 73/1 electro-diesel locomotives marshalled at the country end of formations, whilst on the London end is a specially built GLV (Gatwick luggage van), a rebuild from a 2HAP MBSO car, the work being undertaken at BREL Eastleigh. All former seating has been removed and a luggage storage space constructed together with a guard's office; driving cabs have also been brought up to the latest standard.

The ten GLVs have been allocated numbers 9101-9110 and all 'Gatwick Express' stock is painted in the latest executive livery, and allocated to Stewarts Lane Depot. The 'Gatwick Express' runs every fifteen minutes from 06.00 until 22.00 every day of the week, and takes thirty minutes for the journey, probably providing the finest airport-city link in the world.

Plate 94 (above): After some weeks of satisfactory service the Class 73 locomotives working on the 'Gatwick Express' duties became prone to catching fire, the cause being attributed to a gap in the live rail in the Battersea Park area. Whilst the problem was being sorted out, electric multiple unit stock was substituted on some services and others were hauled/propelled by two Class 73/1 locomotives on diesel power, with a five car 'Gatwick Express' formation and a GLV. One of these makeshift formations, led by GLV No. 9106, with Class 73 locomotives Nos. 73138 and 73140 on the rear, passes Coulsdon North on 7th August 1984.

Colin J. Marsden

Plate 95 (left): All stock for the 'Gatwick Express' service is allocated to Stewarts Lane Depot near Battersea, together with the Class 73 locomotives which operate the service. The average daily diagram for a Class 73 and a nine car formation of Class 488/489 stock is in excess of 800 miles. Class 488/3 unit No. 8302 stands inside Stewarts Lane electric multiple unit depot during the early part of 1984.

Colin J. Marsden

Section B : LMS/BR (LMR), A.C. TYPES

Class 304

For operation on the 'new' electrified Crewe to Manchester section of the London Midland Region, a fleet of 15 four coach electric multiple units was constructed at the BR workshops, Wolverton, and placed in traffic from the early 1960s. These sets collected their power from the 6.25/25kV overhead live wire via a pantograph mounted on one of the intermediate vehicles.

During the late 1950s and early 1960s, Wolverton Works constructed a number of electric multiple fleets which were based on a standard external design but incorporating a number of detail differences. Each four coach Class 304 unit was formed of a Driving Trailer Second (DTS), Motor Brake Second (MBS), Trailer Composite (TC) and a Driving Trailer Brake Second (DTBS), with passenger accommodation provided in the high density mode. All traction and control equipment was housed in and under the MBS coach and traction motors, mounted one on each axle, produce 207hp each, being supplied by BTH. When built, sets were fitted with Germanium rectifiers, but these have subsequently been changed to the Silicon type. The total weight of a four coach set is 152 tons with seating for 19 first and 318 second class passengers. Bogies are of the double bolster type with Gresley knife edge suspension. Numbers allocated are 001-015.

With the extension of the a.c. overhead system, a further twenty units, Nos. 016-035, followed the initial fleet off the production line. Some accommodation alterations were made on these sets mainly in the MBS vehicle, which reduced second class seating to 294.

From the end of 1961, a further fleet of ten units, numbered 036-045, emerged from Wolverton, following the same basic styling as the previous builds.

Since their introduction, Class 304 units have normally operated on the Northern Section of the London Midland Region, receiving maintenance at Allerton, Longsight and Crewe depots. However, their operation into the London Division has been recorded on a number of occasions.

One interesting aspect in the careers of units Nos. 016-023 is worth special mention. When these sets were completed, the Eastern Region were short of units on the Liverpool Street to Shenfield/Southend route, due to their stock receiving conversion to a.c. operation. To overcome this shortage, the London Midland Region sets were loaned to Ilford and this is probably the only occasion that they have ever operated on the 6.25kV a.c. system.

During the early 1980s, sets have received internal alterations at various depots to bring them up to present day standards, including the open plan layout, and the reduction of some sets to three car formations.

Plate 96 (left): In original condition, Class AM4, later Class 304, unit No. 025, arrives at Manchester (London Road) Station in 1961, with a local service from Crewe. In this view, the Driving Trailer Brake Second (DTBS) is leading with the Trailer Composite (TC) coupled behind.

British Rail

Plate 97 (right): A number of alterations have been made to the AM4 fleet over the years, and this now means that all coaches have an open layout, improving passenger comfort. Standing in one of the bay platforms at Manchester (Piccadilly) on 10th January 1981 is set No. 023, in the all blue livery. All sets are now operating in blue/grey Inter-City colours.

Colin J. Marsden

Class 310

For short and medium distance travel at the southern end of the West Coast Main Line electrified network, a fleet of forty nine AM10 or Class 310 units was introduced. Vehicles in these sets did not incorporate the conventional underframe, all load bearing being taken by the integrally-constructed body. This new construction principle not only reduced the weight but increased the room for technical equipment, all of which is accommodated below floor height. Another change from electric multiple unit builds of the period was the provision of air-operated disc brakes. The end design of driving cars was also quite new, being similar to the previously-built Eastern Region Class 309 units, but not having a central door position. Nose end equipment consisting of buck-eye couplings and rubbing plate, air and control jumpers. The four coach formation was: Driving Trailer Second (DTS), Motor Brake Second (MBS), Trailer Second Open (TSO), Driving Trailer Composite (DTC); all vehicles having the open layout. An internal gangway was provided through the unit, except between the brake end of the MBS and the adjoining TSO.

Power and control equipment is mainly housed under the MBS vehicles; traction equipment consisting of four 270hp English Electric traction motors — one mounted on each axle on the motor car. EP contactor control gear and air-cooled silicon rectifiers are also fitted. The total weight of a four coach unit is 158 tons, with passenger accommodation for 25 first and 293 second class. Construction of vehicles took place at Derby, with the first unit emerging in 1965 and the last taking up operation at the beginning of 1967. When delivered, sets were painted in rail blue which, in recent years, has changed to Inter-City blue/grey livery. Set numbers carried are 049-095 which, during the early 1980s, has been prefixed by the three digit TOPS number.

Plate 98 (below): Introduced primarily for operation on the London end section of the electrified West Coast Main Line are the 49 members of Class 310. This view shows unit No. 047, the second of the build, painted in its original colour scheme of all blue with small yellow warning panel on the front, below window height. The photograph was taken from the DTS end. Today, all sets carry Inter-City colours.

GEC Traction Ltd.

Class 317

These four coach units, purpose-built for the controversial Bedford to St. Pancras/Moorgate 'Bed-Pan' line, were built by BREL, and although they owe a considerable amount to the previously-built 1972 design high density stock, a number of design features of the Mk. III passenger vehicles have been included.

Experience has shown the railwy authorities that if a common design structure could be applied to main line, Inter-City and suburban trains, it would be of enormous benefit in terms of reducing production costs. A total of 48 units for the 'Bed-Pan' line, classified 317, was built, each unit being formed of a Driving Trailer Second (DTS), Motor Second (MS), Trailer Second (TS) and a DTS. When built, the TS vehicle was a trailer composite (TC) but the first class accommodation was subsequently declassified; the total passenger loading for a unit being 295. Passenger access is again by twin-leaf sliding doors, two pairs positioned on each side of all vehicles. Power is collected by a roof-mounted pantograph on the MS coach at 25kV a.c., being transrected down to manageable d.c. voltage for traction.

A change from recent electric multiple unit building was that two works were responsible for the construction. York undertook assembly of the driving and motor vehicles, whilst Derby (Litchurch Lane) built the intermediate trailer vehicles. Each coach was constructed from four major assemblies — an underframe, two body ends and a roof, plus six body-side modules; each four coach unit taking some twelve weeks to complete. Once sufficient units were available to the London Midland Region, and lineside equipment was installed, it was the BR Board's intention to introduce the units into public operation, but without the service of a guard, — meaning the train would be operated on a 'driver only' principle. To ensure that all the necessary safety requirements would be fulfilled, a complex system of train to signal box communication was installed, as was the provision of television monitors on station platforms, enabling the driver to watch the full external length of his train. However, at the first mention of dispensing with the guard, and thus improving productivity, the complete railway network was thrown into chaos as the trade unions took industrial action, which eventually led to the entire shut down of the railways, in 1982, for more than a month. Whilst this was taking place, the complete fleet of 48 units was completed and stabled in a number of sidings and yards around the network. Once the very damaging strike was over, and as part of the settlement, the BR Board demanded that 'driver only' operation be introduced without delay. This was carried out and now the system operates quite satisfactorily. After units were placed into service, serious problems were encountered with the underfloor mounted transformers which were found to have a tendency to fall off, as the floor mounting brackets were not strong enough to take the transformer's weight. To overcome this, each unit was sent to BREL Wolverton Works for rectification. To bridge the stock shortage caused on the 'Bed-Pan' line, a number of Eastern Region Class 313 units were loaned to the region.

The Class 317 units, numbered 317301-48, and painted in conventional Inter-City colours, are allocated to Cricklewood Depot.

Plate 99 (left): The Class 317, or 'Bed-Pan' units, were introduced solely for operation on the St. Pancras/Moorgate to Bedford electrified system, and was the first stock designed for driver only operation (DOO). Arriving at St. Pancras, set No. 317311 operates a test special from Bedford on 24th June 1983, and passes the SLOA Pullman set departing with the 'Betjeman Pullman Special', headed by an LMR a.c. electric locomotive.
Colin J. Marsden

Plate 100 (below): Prior to the introduction of Class 317 stock, with the release and closing of passenger doors under the control of the driver, a major industrial dispute prevailed which culminated in a National rail strike called by the drivers' union, ASLEF. The problems were eventually resolved and 'DOO' commenced from late 1983. On 20th January 1984, set No. 317318 approaches Radlett with the 10.50 Bedford to St. Pancras service.
Colin J. Marsden

Lancaster – Morecambe/Heysham Stock

The Midland Railway (MR) had inaugurated its new Irish Sea port at Heysham in September 1904, and had built its own generating station to provide power for the harbour equipment. A steam railmotor shuttled between Heysham and Morecambe where local trains already ran to Lancaster. The area thus provided a suitable site for a limited trial of overhead alternating current electrification, more likely to meet Midland Railway requirements than the existing British conductor rail direct current systems. The London, Brighton & South Coast Railway was looking for the same result through its German-equipped South London line electrification scheme, but although the MR did not authorise its project until 1906, it quickly overtook the LB&SCR and succeeded in running Britain's first a.c. electric trains early in 1908.

Public services commenced between Heysham and Morecambe on 13th April 1908, and were extended to Lancaster (Green Ayre) on 1st July and to the LNWR Castle Station from 14th September, completing a system of 9½ route miles. Electric traction was used only for the local passenger services which were operated by three motor coaches. The power supply was rated at 6,600 volt 25 cycles a.c. Two of the motor coaches had bow collectors, Siemens 180hp motors and electric control, while the third had Westinghouse 150hp motors, a pantograph and electro-pneumatic control. Subsequently, all three cars were fitted with pantographs.

The motor coaches were 60ft. long and 9ft. wide, and the saloons seated 72 passengers on plywood seats. There was a driving compartment at both ends and the motor coaches would always be coupled to one or more of the four control trailer coaches of similar design. These were supplemented by converted Midland Railway clerestory and LMS steel-panelled compartment coaches, so that a variety of train formations could be made up.

The Midland Railway took no further interest in electrification and, after forty years' service, the traction equipment was life-expired, (the power-station had long been replaced by the public supply) so electric services were replaced by steam push and pull trains from 11th February 1951. However, the French were now pioneering electrification at industrial frequency, and it was realised that the Morecambe system could act as a testing place in Britain for its adoption.

The line voltage remained at 6,600 but the frequency was altered to the 50 cycles of the national supply. Much of the Midland Railway overhead was retained, but sections were replaced by prototype structures designed with main line possibilities. Rolling stock for the new system was found by making use of the Siemens-equipped three car sets, built for the Willesden Junction to Earl's Court electrification in 1914 and disused since the withdrawal of this service in 1940. The three sets, converted in 1953, were equipped by English Electric and the fourth followed in 1957 with 'Metrovick' equipment. The a.c. supply was transformed and rectified to operate four 215hp 750 volt d.c. traction motors. In 1955, one train pioneered the use of Germanium rectifiers. The addition of a pantograph and the a.c./d.c. equipment required extensive alterations to the motor coaches and new seating was installed throughout.

Following the re-electrification, frequent regular interval services were provided between Lancaster and Morecambe and a new station was added at Scale Hall, but under the Beeching plan, the duplication of routes between Wennington and Morecambe condemned the Lancaster line to closure from 3rd January 1966.

Plate 102 (right): The new electrified railway was suitable for trial running from November 1952, with regular passenger services commencing during the following August. This picture shows a three coach set from the power car end posing at Morecambe Promenade Station.

GEC Traction Ltd.

Plate 103 (left): The complete 50 cycle route was powered from a new sub-station situated near Lancaster (Green Ayre) Station, collecting its outside power from the North Western Electricity Board supply. A three car set, with driving trailer No. M29022M, stands at Lancaster (Green Ayre) Station while testing was in progress during the early part of 1953.

Author's Collection

Plate 104 (below): When the Lancaster – Morecambe – Heysham line was first electrified in 1908, two coach Midland Railway-built trains were used. Each two coach set was formed of an open motor coach (nearest in view) and a compartment trailer. The total seating capacity for a set was 128. A two coach set, led by motor coach No. 2236 is seen at Lancaster Castle during the 1920s.

J. N. Faulkner Collection

ate 101 (left): During the early 1950s, the ailway Executive was interested in developing e 50 cycle industrial frequency a.c. power stem, and a decision was made to convert e 1908 electrified Lancaster to Morecambe/ eysham line as a full-sized test bed. Stock as provided in the shape of three redundant ondon Division suburban electric multiple units, eavily rebuilt with the aid of the English Electric mpany. Two driving rectifier cars are seen der conversion in this view.

Author's Collection

Section C : LMS/BR (LMR), D.C. TYPES
Liverpool Overhead Stock

The Liverpool Overhead Railway (LOR) was a pioneer venture. It followed the City & South London as the second urban electric railway in Britain and it was the first overhead electric railway in the world. It was equipped with the first electric automatic signalling, and in 1921 these semaphores were replaced by the first daylight colour light signals in Britain.

Fifteen two car trains were supplied by the Electric Construction Corporation for the opening of its initial section from Alexandra Dock to Herculaneum on 6th March 1893. These vehicles were built by Brown, Marshall & Co. Ltd. (predecessors of Metro-Cammell) with teak bodies, each 45ft. long and 8ft. 6in. wide; seating was for 41 second and 16 first class passengers. Both vehicles in the 'set' were motor cars, Nos. 1-30, and each was equipped with a 60hp direct drive motor. Twelve trains were needed to maintain the five minute service.

The extension to Seaforth Sands, which opened on 30th April 1894, required four additional two car trains. These came from the same builders and were numbered 31-38 and they were identical except for a reduced length of 40ft. The line was then extended southwards from Herculaneum Dock to Dingle, from 21st December 1896, and to cope with the growing traffic, the builder supplied vehicles to convert the existing 19 two car sets into fifteen two car and eight three car trains.

This comprised eight second class motor coaches, Nos. 39-46, with 70hp motors and eight 32ft. long first class trailers. Motor coaches Nos. 31-38 were converted for all second occupation to match.

The overall journey time of 32 minutes for the 6½ mile run was now exposed to competition from the city's electric tramways, and it was decided to re-equip the stock with more powerful motors supplied by Dick, Kerr & Co. of Preston. Each motor coach was provided with two 100hp geared motors, enabling an accelerated service, with a 20 minute timing to be inaugurated from September 1902. During the conversion, full width driving cabs were also installed and ten of the original motor coaches were rebuilt with 9ft. 4in. wide bodies to provide five-a-side seating in some of the two car trains.

From 2nd July 1905, the service was extended, mainly over L&YR tracks, from Seaforth Sands to Seaforth and Litherland, on the Liverpool to Southport electrified route. To facilitate through running, the Liverpool Overhead Railway conductor rail was moved from the central to the outside position, and its second class accommodation was redesignated as third to conform to L&YR practice. Once a year, on Grand National day, the LOR trains ran through Aintree over the L&YR tracks.

Gradually the remaining two car trains were strengthened to three car by the building of five new Metro-Cammell trailers, during 1916-18, and by the conversion, between 1932 and 1936, of the five remaining motor coaches of the 31-38 series (two of these had been destroyed in the disastrous fire at Dingle in 1901).

The 100hp motors and the accelerated service had increased power consumption and maintenance costs, so from 1920 onwards they were replaced by lighter 75hp motors. Latterly, the weekday journey time for the seven miles from Dingle to Seaforth & Litherland was 31 minutes.

Liverpool Overhead Railway stock offered third class travellers slatted wooden seats, slam doors and unheated carriages — only the first class provided leather upholstery. To meet post-1945 standards of comfort, the company started to rebuild its stock in its own workshops and, at the rate of one per year, seven trains were modernised. Aluminium panelling covered the wood framing, power-operated doors were fitted, the motorman's compartment was remodelled and upholstery was provided for both classes. The conversion programme was overtaken by the closure of the railway which took place on 31st December 1956. One of the original motor coaches is preserved in the Merseyside County Museum.

Plate 105 (left): The Liverpool Overhead railway began public service on 6th March 1893 when the section between Alexandra Dock and Herculaneum Dock was opened. This was followed during the next three years by the remainder of the network. One of the original two car sets, strengthened to three coaches, stands at James Street Station, one of the busiest on the line, in August 1954.

Colin Boocock

Plate 106 (right): Although the Liverpool Overhead stock looked like multiple unit sets, it was, in fact, unable to operate in multiple, and therefore trains of only three coach formations could be used. In August 1954 one of the rebuilt sets arrives at James Street Station with a Seaforth Sands to Dingle train.

Colin Boocock

PASSENGERS MUST NOT CROSS THE LINE

Class 501

The d.c. electrified network of the London Division tracks of the London Midland Region's Euston to Watford line, including the Richmond to Broad Street North London line, date from 1914. By the late 1950s, the original stock was up for replacement and new stock was sought for the services culminating in this fleet of 'shoe' pick-up 630 volt d.c. electrics.

For the Euston to Watford, Richmond to Broad Street services, 57 three car units were required. These were built by the railway's own workshops at Eastleigh on frames supplied by Ashford. Due to tight loading restrictions all vehicles were constructed on short 57ft. frames. The external body appearance was typical of the period and closely resembled the EPB stock of the SR; the three vehicles of each set being screw-coupled together, fitted with electro-pneumatic brake equipment and equipped for four rail operation (this was later altered to three). Set formations were: Motor Brake Second Open (MBSO), Trailer Second (TS) and Driving Trailer Brake Second Open (DTBSO). Both the MBSO and DTBSO vehicles were of similar layout with a full width driving cab followed by a guard's/luggage compartment. Passengers were accommodated in seven (3 + 2) bays. The TS car was laid out in 9 twelve seat compartments. Total passenger seating capacity for a unit was 256 with a tare weight of 106 tons.

Traction equipment is housed in frame-hung boxes under the MBSO vehicle, with traction motors of the 185hp GEC type being mounted one on each axle of the same car. As these units were of 'high density' style, passenger doors were located by each seating bay; drop light windows being barred to prevent passengers hanging out, as only limited clearances prevailed at a number of locations. Unit ends closely followed the EPB style and incorporated a two character alpha numerical headcode. Control jumpers were housed on the body front while air connections were positioned below buffer height. In common with LMR d.c. stock, no unit numbers were carried when introduced, but sets were formed of like numbered cars; for example 61133, 75133, 70133.

When introduced in 1957/8, all sets were painted in green livery which subsequently changed to blue from the late 1960s. In 1980, a start was made on semi-modernising the sets by opening out the compartment trailer and applying new upholstery. At the same time, sets were repainted in blue/grey livery and given six digital set numbers. All units were allocated to Croxley Green and withdrawn from operation in May 1985.

Plate 107 (above): Looking very much like the SR EPB builds of the 1950s were these three coach LMR London District Class 501 units. This view shows unit No. 135, formed of cars M61135, M70135, M75135, when new. The motor coach is nearest to the camera and shows the mass of under-floor equipment carried by these vehicles. The livery shown in this picture is BR electric multiple unit green, with yellow numbering and lettering.
Author's Collection

Plate 108 (left): The Class 501 units remained in operation until May 1985, when they were replaced by Class 416 (EPB) stock on the Richmond line and by Class 313 stock on the Euston to Watford section. A three car formation with MBSO No. M61141 leading, descends under the LMR a.c. lines near Wembley whilst working a Watford to Euston train on 12th May 1980.

Colin J. Marsden

Class 502

This fleet of Liverpool to Southport/Ormskirk stock was constructed at Derby by the LMS in 1939/41 to replace original stock of 1904 vintage.

The line which, in recent years, has become known as the 'Northern Line' is electrified at 630 volt d.c., with pick-up via the third rail system. Stock was of similar appearance to that of the Wirral Class 503 units, detailed in the next section. A total of 152 cars was built — 59 Motor Brake Second Open (MBSO), 50 Trailer Second Open (TSO), 9 Trailer Composite Open (TCO) and 34 Driving Trailer Composite Open (DTCO). Vehicles were formed into 34 three car units formed MBSO, TSO, DTCO, and 25 two coach sets formed either MBSO-TSO or MBSO-TCO. These formations meant that the two car sets only had a driving position at one end and therefore had to be coupled to another set for public service. The dimensions for all vehicles were 66ft. 6in. long by 9ft. 6in. wide. Their construction was not totally conventional as the bodies were not carried on a frame, but the body itself acted as a load-bearing tubular structure. Internal layout of vehicles was in the high density styling of 2 + 3 in second class areas and 2 + 2 in the first class; passenger access being by air-operated double-leaf sliding doors. Traction and control equipment, all housed in the MBSO, was supplied by English Electric; third rail collector shoes being fitted at both ends of power cars but not on any other vehicle. The MBSO cars were close-coupled to the adjoining vehicles but all other coupling was of the screw-shackle type. Outer ends of trailer cars were fitted with an observation window and a signal button, used for shunting movements, these being necessary as a driving position was not provided at both ends of all fixed sets.

Normally, stock remained in the intended formations, but in later years some alterations were carried out, including coupling driving trailer vehicles to two car sets. After many years of service, the nine TCO vehicles were rebuilt, some into TSOs and others into DTCOs. A number of vehicles were withdrawn during the 1960s and early 1970s mainly as surplus to operating requirements, leaving a total of 36 three car and 7 two car units still in service by 1973.

The Class 502 units remained in service until 1981 when all vehicles were withdrawn. Again, in common with LMS d.c. unit policy, no unit numbers were carried, but formations usually remained constant for lengthy periods.

Plate 109 (left): Displaying its original LMS maroon livery, a three car formation of Liverpool to Southport stock stands in sidings at Meols Cop during 1940. The vehicle nearest to the camera an MBSO, with all traction and control equipment mounted between the bogies. Note the third class notion on the saloon windows.

Author's Collection

Plate 110 (below): The new Liverpool Loop line service (underground) was introduced from 1977, serving stations St. James, Moorfields, Lime Street and Central. Car No. M29890M leads a formation bound for Kirkby, at Moorfields soon after the line opened.

Colin J. Marsden

Class 503

The first Class 503 units were ordered by the LMS during 1938, and a total of 19 three car sets was built for use on the Liverpool (Central) 650 volt d.c. system. All vehicles were constructed on short frames and had a non-standard width of 9ft. 11in. over stepboards. Sets were formed of a Motor Brake Second Open (MBSO), Trailer Composite Open (TCO) and a Driving Trailer Second Open (DTSO). Construction of the vehicles was not carried out by the LMS but by the Metropolitan Carriage, Wagon & Finance Company and the Birmingham Railway Carriage & Wagon Company Ltd. Passenger accommodation was in the 2 + 2 layout in second class carriages and 2 + 1 in the first class portion; passenger access being by air-operated sliding doors, two pairs on either side of each vehicle. When these sets were designed, great emphasis was steered towards a modern look and, wherever possible, sharp corners were replaced by curves which gives the units a very pleasing appearance. Unit ends incorporated three windows with a roller blind destination indicator at the centre top; route and frontal marker indications being provided by four white lights, one of which being fitted with a red hinged lense, acting as a tail light when required. Other frontal equipment consisted of air brake/main reservoir connections on the nose end, while control jumpers were mounted under drawgear height. No buffers were fitted and all buffing and traction forces were transmitted via a buck-eye coupler. Within units, vehicles were close-coupled. Power collection being by conventional shoes mounted on the outer ends of driving cars, all traction equipment was housed under the MBSO. Main traction equipment consisted of four 135hp English Electric traction motors, one mounted on each axle of the MBSO. One interesting fitting on this stock was a 'trip-cock' device; if a train passed a danger signal an arm on the lineside activated a trip on the train and made an emergency application of the train's brakes. Each three car unit weighed 77 tons and had accommodation for 40 first and 141 second class passengers, but from the summer of 1971, first class accommodation was removed.

In 1956/7, further 'new' stock was required for the Liverpool d.c. network to replace the aged Mersey Railway stock. Twenty four sets were ordered for this purpose, plus four units as replacement to stock damaged by enemy action in 1941. This stock was constructed by the same manufacturers as previously, and was of very similar external appearance, but a major difference was the fitting of an MG set to provide a 50 volt supply for control and lighting circuits. Other minor detail differences existed, such as the frame design and body ribbing.

From 1972, a start was made to fit end doors on the driving cars for use on the new tunnel section of the route, (this being a Department of Transport requirement for stock used on lengthy tunnel sections). This alteration made it necessary to completely amend the front end layout of cars, and fix duplication air connections on either side of the door.

Following the introduction of 1972-designed high density electric multiple units, progressively from the late 1970s, the Class 503 units have been slowly withdrawn, the final units operating in mid-1985.

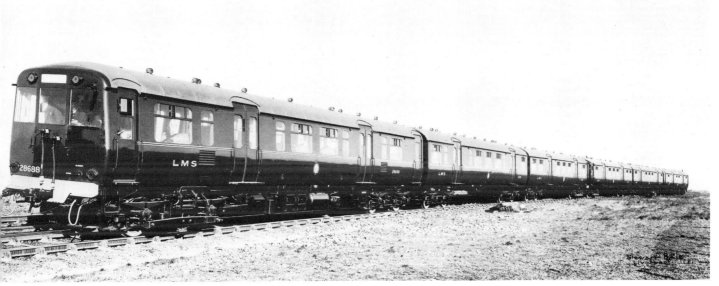

Plate 111 (above): Being very similar in appearance to the previously shown Class 502 sets are these Class 503 units, introduced from 1938 for the Liverpool suburban network. A six car formation, made up of 2 three car units, is pictured in 'as built' condition, painted in LMS maroon livery.

GEC Traction Ltd.

Plate 112 (left): Over the years, the 1938 and 1956 built stock passed through works when various repaints took place, taking the vehicles into BR green, BR blue, and finally blue/grey livery. From 1972, a start was made to fitting emergency end doors to driving cars, which was necessary to comply with DOT regulations on stock traversing tunnel sections. MBS No. M28376M is seen at the now closed BREL Horwich Works in 1981 awaiting an overhaul.

Colin J. Marsden

Class 504

The electrified route from Manchester (Victoria) to Bury dates from 1916 when the Lancashire & Yorkshire Railway introduced an electrically-operated passenger service. The stock under review in this section was introduced from 1959 as replacement for these original formations.

The route from Manchester (Victoria) to Bury is an isolated electrified network having no electrified branches. Depot facilities exist at Bury and electrification is by the 1,200 volt d.c. third rail system.

The 1959 built stock is still in service today and was constructed at Wolverton Works to typical late 1950 electric multiple unit design. A total of 26 two car sets was built, formed of a Motor Brake Second Open (MBSO) and a Driving Trailer Composite Open (DTCO). The passenger accommodation provided was in MBSO two four bay saloons in the 3 + 2 styling, providing 84 seats. The DTCO vehicles were laid out as driver's cab, four bay second class saloon, two first class compartments and three second class compartments. This composite arrangement lasted until 1962 when the first class accommodation was withdrawn. Later in the 1960s, the internal layout of the now DTS vehicles was rebuilt to all open style. The end connections to the units consisted of a buck-eye coupling at drawgear height, with air and control cables positioned on the nose end — thus removing the need for staff to work near the 1,200 volt live rail. Traction and control equipment is all housed in the MBSO vehicle and traction motors are of the 141hp type and mounted on each axle of the MBSO vehicle, and are supplied by English Electric.

Due to the non-standard nature of the system, these units are unable to operate on any other routes. No set numbers are carried by this stock but again pairs of vehicles operate together for extended periods. Car numbers allocated are as follows: MBSO — 65436-61; DTSO — 77157-82. Services are usually formed of one two car set but, during peak periods, four car formations are used. When built, the stock was painted in green livery but this subsequently changed in the late 1960s to BR rail blue, which in more recent years again changed to blue/grey.

Plate 113 (right): The new and present stock for the Manchester to Bury line, equipped with its unique 1,200 volt d.c. third rail system, emerged in 1959, and conformed to the standard electric multiple unit design of the period. A four coach train, formed of 2 two car sets, led by driving trailer No. M77158, is illustrated, painted in the BR multiple unit green livery.

Author's Collection

Plate 114 (below): Services on the 9¾ mile Manchester (Victoria) to Bury route are usually formed of single two car sets, providing accommodation for 178 second class passengers, but four car formations operate during peak periods. A set led by DMS No. M65446 arrives at Bury on 3rd October 1981 with the 16.45 train from Manchester (Victoria).

Colin J. Marsden

Class 506

With the electrification of the Manchester to Sheffield/Wath route, in the early 1950s, came the electrification of the Manchester to Glossop line on an identical 1,500 volt d.c. overhead system.

For use on this Manchester suburban route, a fleet of eight three car electric multiple units was constructed; set formations being made up of a Motor Brake Second Open (MBSO), Trailer Composite Open (TCO) and a Driving Trailer Second Open (DTSO). Passenger accommodation was provided in both longitudinal and transverse arrangements; MBSO and DTSO cars seating 52 and 60 second class passengers respectively, and the TCO seating 24 first and 38 second class travellers. In the early 1960s, first class accommodation was withdrawn, thus increasing the total second class seating to 174 per unit. Construction of the DTSO cars was carried out by the Birmingham Railway Carriage & Wagon Company Ltd., whilst the MBSO and TCO vehicles were provided by Metropolitan Cammell Ltd. Power and control equipment was supplied by GEC and mounted under the MBSO. Electro-pneumatic brake equipment was also fitted, as were screw couplers on the unit ends, cars within each set being close-coupled.

Stock commenced operation in June 1954, with the eight sets housed at the new d.c. depot at Reddish and, from then until late 1984, they have operated on the Manchester to Glossop line, providing BR with a remarkably reliable unit.

Following the closure of the Manchester to Sheffield, via Woodhead, route from the early 1980s, the Manchester to Glossop section was the only remaining 1,500 volt d.c. system on British Rail. The depot at Reddish was subsequently closed and maintenance of the Class 506 units was transferred to Longsight.

The d.c. lines were re-equipped for a.c. operation in 1984 and the Class 506 stock was withdrawn. No unit numbers were carried, but sets were always formed of like numbered cars, e.g. 59401, 59501, 59601. When introduced, sets were painted in green livery which later changed to BR blue, and in recent years changed again to Inter-City blue/grey colours.

Plate 115 (left): At a quick glance, these LMR/ER Class 506 Manchester to Glossop sets could be mistaken for the BR(GE) Class 306 suburban units. This view, probably photographed soon after the route was electrified, shows a three car set at Hadfield, forming a service to Manchester (London Road).

British Rail

Plate 116 (below): Although the majority of the 1,500 volt d.c. system was abolished during the early 1980s, the 15¾ mile Manchester to Hadfield line remained until 1984, units receiving maintenance at Longsight a.c. depot. Two Class 506 sets Nos. M59402M and M59401M stand between duties at Manchester (Piccadilly) on 10th January 1981. Note the joint BR/Greater Manchester Transport symbols on the body side.

Colin J. Marsden

Class 507

Another of the 1972 stock derivatives are these three car Class 507 units, built for operation on the Merseyrail network, around the suburbs of Liverpool and being allocated to Hall Road Depot.

These 33 units were introduced from 1978, and were built at BREL's York Works as part of the production run including Classes 313, 314, 315 and 508. Each unit is formed of a Battery Motor Brake Second (BMBS), Trailer Second Open (TSO), and a Motor Brake Second (MBS). Passenger accommodation is in the high density 3 + 2 open layout and each coach has two pairs of double-leaf sliding doors on each side. The total seating for a three car unit is 232, with sufficient room for more than 100 standing. Traction equipment is mounted on both bogies of each driving car and consists of eight 110hp English Electric traction motors. Although the majority of 1972 designed production units were geared for passenger operation of doors, under the overall control of the guard, the Class 507 units were not provided with the individual door control by each door, meaning that the guard has to open all the train doors at each station. To meet local requirements, a wider than normal step was provided by each door position rendering the units as slightly non-standard.

In common with other 1972 type stock, fully automatic couplers are fitted under the control of the driver by push buttons, with a central tightlock coupling taking all traction forces, with an associated electrical/air connection box below.

Following the reallocation of the Class 508 units to the Merseyrail system from the Southern Region, these two classes will form the backbone of motive power on Merseyside for a number of years to come.

Plate 117 (below): The replacement stock for the aged Class 502/3 units in the Liverpool area came in the early 1980s, when Class 507 and 508 stock was introduced. The Class 507 units are allocated to Hall Road Depot, Liverpool, and usually operate only in three car formations. On 19th September, set No. 507014 arrives at Ormskirk with the 14.59 service from Liverpool (Central).

Brian Morrison

Class 508

After successful testing of the prototype high density stock on the Southern Region, production sets of various types were authorised. By the late 1970s, the SR were getting desperate for new rolling stock and were given the 43 strong Class 508 fleet as a stop-gap until purpose-built SR replacement stock was made available. The Class 508 units were four car sets and formed of a Driving Motor Second (DMS), Trailer Second (TS), TS and DMS. The basic design followed the PEP styling with both coach and internal layout, and sliding doors were again fitted, but with passenger push button control. Power equipment, supplied by GEC, in the shape of one 110hp traction motor to each axle, was fitted to the driving cars only. Braking was the standard EP type with additional rheostatic (dynamic) brakes on power cars. The passenger accommodation, set out in the high density mode, provided seats for 74 in DMS and 84 in TS cars. However, the coach is designed to take an equal number of people standing.

The first Class 508 units were delivered to the SR in the autumn of 1979, and after commissioning and training, commenced passenger operation from 17th December 1979, sets progressively replacing aged suburban units as they were delivered. After a short period of service,

some problems were encountered with wheel slip/slide protection equipment, which reduced brake pressure or cut off power if any indication of wheel slip/slide was detected by the unit. Unfortunately, this equipment was not totally satisfactory, and for a lengthy period set No. 508002 operated under test conditions to seek a remedy for the problem, which was eventually overcome by fitting a wheel slip protection override button.

Class 508 livery was blue/grey, from new, with full yellow warning ends and black cab window surrounds. Another break from previous SR practice was the omission of the two digit route indicator and the fitting of a route destination panel.

By November 1981, the SR stock position eased, and two units, Nos. 508042/3 were reduced to three car formations and transferred to the London Midland Region at Birkenhead to operate on their intended route. Sets Nos. 508039-41 followed in February 1983, and the remainder of the fleet by December 1984 as Class 455 units were introduced. The sets are now all allocated to Birkenhead and operate in three car formations on Liverpool suburban duties.

Plate 118 (below): A picture that cannot be repeated — a Class 508 electric multiple unit operating on the SR. These four coach 1972-designed high density units were used on the SR from 1979 until the delivery of the full complement of Class 455 stock during late 1984. No. 508002 was photographed at Weybridge on 1st June 1983 working the 18.00 train to Staines, and was transferred to Liverpool during June 1984 for use on the Merseyrail network.

Colin J. Marsden

Mersey Railway Stock

The under-river section of the Mersey Railway was opened on 1st February 1886, and extensions to Birkenhead Park, Rock Ferry and Liverpool (Central) followed between 1888 and 1892. However, the high hopes of the promoters were quickly dashed as steam traction on the 1 in 27 gradients through the tunnels created a foul atmosphere with filthy stations and trains. Self-respecting travellers were therefore deterred, and declining revenues forced the company into receivership.

Unable to finance its own electrification, the Mersey Railway was rescued by the Westinghouse company of the USA, which was eager to obtain a foothold in the British market by carrying out the conversion from its own resources. Work was quickly accomplished, without any interruption to traffic, and the inaugural electric service ran on 3rd May 1903.

To operate the five mile system, 57 cars of typical American styling were provided, featuring clerestory roofs, matchboarded sides, manually-operated end gates and longitudinal seats — rattan-covered in firsts and bare wooden sheet for third class posteriors. Bodywork was by George F. Milnes & Company and the cars were erected at the Trafford Park Works of British Westinghouse. A total of 24 cars was powered and 33 were trailers, and both types were built in first and third class versions as well as five composite trailers. Each motor coach was powered by four 100hp Westinghouse-geared motors, and control was on the multiple unit principle, using remote controlled drum controllers, the first time in Britain that this system had been adopted. Curiously, the trains carried no air compressors for their Westinghouse brakes, and the reservoirs had to be charged at the termini.

A service of twenty trains per hour was provided under the river, divided equally between the Rock Ferry and Birkenhead Park branches. It was soon found desirable to reduce the length of the normal five car trains during off peak hours, and to enable this to be done easily all the trailers were converted to control trailers, between 1904 and 1907 and, with four additional trailers from Milnes, Voss & Company in 1908, it became possible to cut each five car train down to a three car formation. On alternate days, it was the turn of the Liverpool or the Birkenhead end's two cars to be detached. Gradually, the open platforms were replaced by closed vestibules, and the gatemen were made redundant.

Between 1921 and 1924, automatic colour light signalling and automatic terminal working at Liverpool (Central) increased line capacity on the under-river section to thirty trains per hour. To provide additional stock, Cravens of Sheffield built one complete five car train and two spare composite motor coaches. With elliptical roofs and domed ends, these vehicles differed from the original stock, but were operationally compatible. Electrical equipment was by Metropolitan Vickers, with four 125hp motors in each power car.

In 1936 the platforms and reversing siding at Liverpool (Central) were extended for six car trains and, to provide this strengthening, the Gloucester Railway Carriage & Wagon Company Ltd. supplied ten third class trailers, similar in appearance to the Cravens stock, but of steel consruction.

Since electrification, connection with the steam trains of the Wirral Railway, and later the LMS to New Brighton and West Kirby, had been by interchange at Birkenhead Park. It was now planned to electrify these lines and run through services to and from Liverpool (Central). To adapt the Mersey Railway for this extension, its conductor rail was moved to the standard position. With plans to operate services in the Wirral with Mersey stock, this was fitted with compressors, train heating, rearranged and upholstered seating, deadman equipment, and changeover switches for third rail/fourth rail systems. Wirral electrification commenced on 14th March 1938, and the normal practise on weekdays was for Mersey Railway stock to run to Rock Ferry and New Brighton, while on Sundays it went to West Kirby. This was arranged to maintain route knowledge among the train crews of both companies.

Wartime bombing on Merseyside destroyed or damaged four of the company's vehicles and they were rebuilt or replaced in the style of the 1936 Gloucester stock. Enemy action fortunately did not require the service of the four ex-Hammersmith & City six car trains, which were refurbished by London Transport for emergency use.

The Mersey Railway was absorbed by the London Midland Region of British Railways on 1st January 1948. With most of the Mersey stock half a century old, modernisation in the 1950s provided for its replacement by 24 three car electric multiple units similar to the 19 LMS Wirral units of 1938 (today's Class 503). First of all, the Mersey section had to be converted to third rail operation in 1955. Delivery of the new stock commenced in July 1956, and the last Mersey Railway trains were withdrawn in March 1957. Unfortunately, a fire at Derby Works destroyed the example which had been chosen for preservation.

Plate 119 (above): Following wartime losses to Mersey Railway stock, replacements were built by the Gloucester Railway Carriage & Wagon Company in 1936. This view shows 1936 Gloucester driving trailer third No. 105, and although painted in BR livery and slightly modernised, it remained in service until 1957.

British Rail

Plate 120 (right): Looking, with its clerestory roof, more like something from the American Railroad than a British train, is this Mersey Railway three car fourth rail electric unit arriving at Birkenhead (Central) from Rock Ferry. Motor first car No. 10 leads the three car set, constructed in 1903 by G. F. Milnes & Co. of Hadley, Shropshire, and although slightly altered and repainted on nationalisation, it remained in service for many years.

W. Hubert Foster

Liverpool to Southport Stock

Liverpool's third electric railway was the Lancashire & Yorkshire Railway's (L&YR) commuter line from Liverpool (Exchange) Station to Southport. Some electric trains commenced public service from 22nd March 1904, but troubles at the Formby power house caused their temporary withdrawal, and it was not until 13th May that full electric operation commenced. In addition to the main line, electric traction was extended to the first three miles of the West Lancashire line from Southport to Preston as far as Crossens from 5th April 1904, to provide a local service to Southport's suburbs. Electrification was on the 650 volt d.c. third rail system, although, in its early years, the path for the return current was assisted by a fourth rail bonded to the running rails.

Rolling stock comprised 56 clerestory-roofed vehicles built at the L&YR's Newton Heath Works, with electrical equipment being supplied by Dick, Kerr & Co. — four 150hp traction motors powered each motor coach, with direct control of the motors. An unusual feature of the L&YR stock was that it employed the vacuum brake, a rare fitting on electric stock. The coaches were 60ft. long and 10ft. wide, the widest ever to run in Britain. Accommodation was in saloons with recessed doors, and originally the motor coaches had tapered ends. The extreme width made opening windows hazardous, and ventilation was originally confined to vents in the clerestory, but soon upper lights were added and some passenger-controlled fans were fitted, and finally came some opening windows for emergency use only.

The 28 motor coaches seated 69 third class passengers on rattan-covered reversible seats, while the 28 first class trailers accommodated 66 passengers on tapestry-covered seats in panelled saloons. Initially, four car trains were run — motor, trailer, trailer, motor — but this provided too much first class accommodation for even the prosperous residents of Southport. In 1905, therefore, two additional motor coaches and 12 third class trailers seating 80 passengers were built, and five car trains became the rule. In later years some of the original stock was re-equipped with more non-reversible seats (92 in these trailers) and, as travellers find in present day BR stock, the seats no longer corresponded to the windows.

Additional traffic required the construction, in 1905/6, of eight motor coaches of a slightly modified design; six first class trailers and the same number of third class trailers. Two of the original motor coaches, which had been wrecked in a disastrous collision at Hall Road in July 1905, were also rebuilt to the new design. In 1910, two of the third class trailers were converted to control trailers. The final addition to the direct control stock was six third class motor coaches, built in 1913/14, to the current pattern of 63ft. 7in. length with elliptical roofs.

Meanwhile, the electrified mileage had been expanding; the loop from Marsh Lane on the Southport line to Aintree from 1st June 1906, the direct line to Aintree on the following 7th December, onwards to Maghull from 1st October 1909, to Town Green on 3rd July 1911 and finally to Ormskirk from 12th July 1913. These lines were mainly worked by a new generation of multiple unit control stock incompatible with the direct control type — 12 third motor coaches, which retained the clerestory roofs but were fitted with gangways at the outer ends and half width cabs. The original direct control stock was vestibuled only within each unit. These motor coaches, built in 1907/8, were split between vehicles, with or without luggage compartments, and were accompanied by six third class trailers.

Construction standards now changed to coaches 63ft. 7in. long with elliptical roofs. From 1910 to 1914 the provision of 7 first class and 23 third class trailers, 4 driving trailer thirds and 8 motor coaches with double-ended cabs and luggage compartments was made; the later examples with 250hp traction motors. The multiple unit stock was thus capable of being made up into a more flexible variety of formations.

A short link between Seaforth & Litherland and Seaforth Sands (LOR) had been opened on 2nd July 1905 and, from 2nd February 1906 to the outbreak of World War I, the L&YR operated an hourly through service from Southport to Dingle. To conform to LOR restrictions, special light-weight stock, only 45ft. long, was built at Newton Heath. The cars, twelve in number, were all motored with two 125hp units, and cabs at each end. Accommodating 70 passengers in both classes, they could run singly or coupled two or three together. After the withdrawal of the through service to the LOR, they operated a workmen's service to Gladstone Dock (L&YR), between 1914 and 1924, but latterly spent most of their time on the Crossens local service and lingered there as late as 1945.

Two baggage cars, with bench seats for workmen, were built at Newton Heath in 1903/4 and were equipped with two 150hp traction motors; a third car with multiple unit control facilities was added in 1921. One of the original cars was destroyed by bombing in 1941, but the other two outlasted the passenger stock and were withdrawn in 1952.

The L&YR provided over 60 trains a day between Liverpool and Southport with additional short workings to Hall Road. The standard timing to Southport was around 37 minutes, but the non-stop residential expresses took only 25 minutes. There was some easing of these schedules between the wars, but the arrival of the new LMS stock in 1940 (BR Class 502) restored a 40 minute journey time. The L&YR stock was then gradually withdrawn, and had all gone by 1942.

The annual Grand National race meeting attracted very heavy traffic to Aintree, and to provide additional rolling stock for the electric service, the L&YR, in 1910, converted three trains of ten 6-wheeled coaches to run between two of the direct control motor coaches. The LMS replaced these with three trains of five mixed LNWR and MR bogie compartment coaches. For a time, in 1923, a train of 5 L&YR bogie coaches was converted to electric operation by the addition of a 150hp motor under each brake van.

The latter may have been a trial for the compartment stock introduced by the LMS on the Ormskirk line in 1926/7. Eleven three car trains were built; motor coach thirds by Metropolitan Carriage & Wagon Company with four 265hp Metrovick traction motors, trailer composites by the Clayton Wagon Company, and driving trailer thirds by the Midland Railway Carriage & Wagon Company. Five of the trailer composites were transferred to the Manchester South Junction & Altrincham line in 1939, and the stock was reformed into three car and two car units to make up standard five coach trains to work alongside the new LMS stock. One of the two coach sets was converted to parcels service in 1952, to be replaced by an Eastleigh-built motor luggage van, transferred from Tyneside in 1964. The same year saw the withdrawal of the remaining 1926/7 stock, which had about the same life span as the similar units in the London area.

One item of curiosity is worthy of note. In 1912, the L&YR built, at Horwich, an electric locomotive on the frames of a 2-4-2T. Powered by four 150hp motors, it was equipped with both bow collectors and shoes. For about two years it worked transfer trips with coal traffic between Aintree Sorting Sidings and North Mersey Yard over the third rail of the loop line to Aintree, and used its overhead collector in the shunting yards.

Plate 121 (right): During 1953, two single baggage cars were introduced to replace L&YR-built vehicles. These cars were formed from two redundant compartment cars of 1926/7 vintage. The two single vehicles remained in service some years after other compartment stock was withdrawn, and were still active in 1964. This official view shows baggage car No. 28497, with its power equipment end nearest to the camera.

British Rail

Plate 122 (above): Carrying London & North Western Railway (LNWR) livery and crests, a seven car formation of camshaft control stock is seen at Meols Cop during 1922. This set would have operated as a seven car formation during 'peak' periods, but in off peak hours the two leading vehicles, Nos. 3051 and 3100, would have been detached.

British Rail

Plate 123 (below): This view, photographed from the opposite end of the same train as the previous illustration, depicts third class clerestory motor coach No. 3045, introduced in 1907; coupled to this is 1904 first class clerestory trailer No. 421. Note the power pick-up shoes on the trailer as well as on the motor vehicle.

British Rail

Holcombe Brook Branch Stock

The electrification of this steeply-graded 3¾ mile single line branch was carried out at the expense of Dick, Kerr & Co., the Preston electrical engineering firm, which later formed part of English Electric. They proposed to tender for a contract in Brazil using the unfamiliar system of 3,500 volt d.c. overhead supply, and required a convenient line on which to carry out development work and trials. Following Dick, Kerr's part in the Liverpool area electrification, the Lancashire & Yorkshire Railway (L&YR) made the Holcombe Brook branch available to the firm.

After preliminary trials, electric trains replaced the steam rail motor in public service from 29th July 1913. The L&YR built four coaches at its Newton Heath Works — two motor coaches and two driving trailers. The motor coaches were powered by four Dick, Kerr electric traction motors, one car at 150hp and the other at 250hp, operating at 1750 volt d.c. connected permanently in parallel. Current collection was via two pantographs on the motor coach.

The Holcombe Brook cars were similar in appearance to the later Liverpool area stock and accomodated third class passengers only — 75 in the motor coach and 85 in the trailer. Folding side steps were provided for the benefit of travellers ascending/descending from and to the rail-level halts on the branch.

Dick, Kerr & Co. had completed their trials by 1916 and, as the Bury to Manchester line was now being electrified on the 1,200 volt side contact third rail system, it was decided to convert the Holcombe Brook branch to the same system. However, before conversion was complete, the 3,500 volt power supply failed in 1917 and, for a time, 1,200 volts was fed into the overhead at Bury, picked up by the pantographs of a 3,500 volt car and passed by cable to the motors of a permanently-coupled 1,200 volt car. Final conversion to the third rail system was completed on 29th March 1918.

The 3,500 volt stock was laid aside for several years but was utilised again in 1927 for an early experiment in diesel-electric traction. One of the motor coaches was fitted with a 500hp Beardmore diesel engine and an associated English Electric generator and other equipment and, combined with the other vehicles, this formed a four car train which worked on the local service between Blackpool (Central) and Lytham during 1928/29.

The short Holcombe Brook branch was vulnerable to road competition, and when the power supply equipment became life-expired, electric services were withdrawn from 25th March 1951 and the replacement steam push-pull trains soon followed on 7th May 1952.

Plate 124 (below):   This rare illustration shows a three car Dick, Kerr electric unit on the 3¾ mile long Holcombe Brook line, probably photographed around 1920. The overhead line on this original electrified project was at 3,500 volt d.c. but, by 1917, the line was converted to third rail pick-up at 1,200 volt d.c.

GEC Traction Ltd.

Manchester to Bury Stock

The Lancashire & Yorkshire Railway (L&YR) had chosen 650 volt d.c. for its third rail electrification on Merseyside, but when the company came to consider the conversion of its steeply-graded suburban lines to the north and east of Manchester, a higher voltage was thought necessary. Clearance problems and complex junctions ruled out overhead wiring, so a unique system was devised of a 1,200 volt d.c. supply through a side contact third rail protected by wooden boards (as on Merseyside, initially there was a fourth rail bonded to the running rails to aid the path of the return current).

The route chosen for the first stage of electrification was the 9½ mile line from Manchester (Victoria) to Bury (Bolton Street), a busy suburban link with six intermediate stations. The company built its own power-station at Clifton Junction, on the line to Bolton, which would have been strategically situated for further extensions. Dick, Kerr & Co. of Preston was responsible for all electrical equipment on the rolling stock, and for much of the generating and sub-station machinery.

The 66 cars for the Bury line were constructed at Newton Heath Works; all were 63ft. 7in. long of all-metal design, steel-framed with aluminium panelling. All cars had half width driving cabs at both ends, 38 of them were third class motor coaches with seating for 74 passengers, 14 were third class trailers with 95 seats, and the other 14 were 72-seater first class trailers. Seating was in long saloons with reversible and fixed seats, with rattan covers for the third class. The motor coaches were powered by four 200hp traction motors. All vehicles were vestibuled at both ends and trains could be made up in a variety of formations, but the normal train was of five cars; motor, third trailer, motor, first trailer, motor.

Delivery of the electric stock was delayed by the demands of war production, and when public electric services started on 17th April 1916, only a partial service could be provided, and it was a further four months before steam trains were completely replaced. Between the wars, two additional stations were opened, and the standard timing became 24 minutes throughout. After 1945, the first class accommodation was reduced and many of the intermediate cabs and vestibule connections were taken out of use. The uneventful history of the Bury electric line was marred by the Irk Valley collision on 15th August 1953, in which ten passengers lost their lives and two cars were totally destroyed, one of them plunging 50ft. from the viaduct into the river below.

After more than 40 years of service, the L&YR electrics were due for replacement and, during 1959/60, they were gradually ousted by the 28 two car sets (now Class 504) built by BR at Wolverton Works. The unique traction supply was retained, although the Clifton Junction Power Station had been closed in 1933. If the question of rolling stock replacement had occurred a few years later, during the Beeching regime, the Manchester to Bury line would probably have shared the fate of the Tyneside system.

Plate 125 (below): A five car formation of 1916 Manchester to Bury stock, led by driving motor third No. 3502, is seen in this illustration photographed around 1924. Note the emergency ladder hung under the far end of the leading coach, and the third and fourth rail layout.

Author's Collection

Plate 126 (above): This view of a five car train of L&YR Manchester to Bury stock is taken in LMS days and shows a Bury to Manchester (Victoria) service led by car No. 28515, departing from Bowker Vale Station which opened in 1935. The roof-mounted indicator box appears to have had its blind removed.

W. Hubert Foster

Plate 127 (right): With 'All stations to Manchester' on its route indicator, a five car formation of original Manchester to Bury stock stands at Radcliffe (Central) around 1953, soon after major reconstruction work had been carried out. Motor car No. M28435 is leading in this view, and it was built as L&YR car No. 3001, later being numbered LMSR No. 14502, and finally to BR No. M28435.

Author's Collection

North Western Electrics

The London North Western Railway (LNWR), in November 1911, announced plans for the electrification of its suburban lines in the London area, including those of the North London Railway. This involved the construction of additional local tracks, known as the 'New Line', between Watford Junction and Camden Town, where a complex system of burrowing junctions would separate the traffic bound for Euston and Broad Street. Earlier plans for a low level terminal loop at Euston were replaced by the extension of the Bakerloo tube line to Queen's Park, and by through running of Underground trains to Watford. The 'New Line' was opened between Willesden Junction and Watford for steam traction during 1912/13, and a new branch was built from Watford to Croxley Green in 1912.

The electrification was at 630 volt d.c. with third and fourth rail supply; a system compatible with that of the Bakerloo, District and Metropolitan lines over which through running was to take place. The LNWR built its own power-station at Stonebridge Park, near Willesden.

The first electric service commenced on 1st May 1914 between Willesden Junction (High Level) and Earl's Court, over the jointly-owned West London Railway. Parts of the route had already been electrified by the Metropolitan and District companies and, for the time being, the power supply was drawn from their sub-stations, and District trains operated the service. The first LNWR electric trains came into service on 22nd November 1914, comprising four three car trains built by the Metropolitan Carriage and Wagon Company, with Siemens electrical equipment, and powered by four 250hp traction motors. Trains consisted of a third class motor coach, composite trailer and driving trailer third, vestibuled throughout and with seating in open saloons with sliding doors at each end. Total accommodation was for 38 first and 138 third class passengers.

The 'New Line' was extended from Willesden to Queen's Park from 10th March 1915, and Bakerloo trains commenced to run through to the 'New Line' station at Willesden Junction, using Underground current. Work on completion of the 'New Line' and the Camden Town junctions had now been suspended due to the outbreak of war, but construction of Stonebridge Park Power-Station continued slowly, and this came into service in February 1916 enabling the LNWR to dispense with power supplies from other companies.

The way was now clear for the inauguration of electric services over the North London line from Broad Street to Richmond and Kew Bridge from 1st October 1916. The LSWR owned the section of line from Gunnersbury to Richmond which was already electrified for District line services. At Willesden, the electrification included the link from Kensal Green Junction to the new station and on to Stonebridge Park car sheds.

For this major extension of the scheme, the well-known 'Oerlikon' stock was built. This comprised 38 three car sets and five spare motor coaches; the motors were built by the Metropolitan Carriage & Wagon Company at Saltley and the trailers at the railway's Wolverton Works. Electrical equipment was supplied by the Swiss firm of Oerlikon, with four 260hp motors to each motor coach. The general layout of the sets was similar to the Siemens stock; one pair of doors was omitted in the motor coaches, and more spacious seating reduced the accommodation to 33 first and 130 third class. Both types of stock were furnished internally to a high standard and were unsurpassed among suburban electrics for their comfortable seating and smooth riding. One of the motor coaches has been preserved in the National Railway Museum, York.

Electric traction was extended over the 'New Line' from Stonebridge Park to Watford Junction on 16th April 1917. The LNWR operated some peak hour electric trains from Broad Street to Watford, and continued to run some steam trains from Euston, but the basic service was provided by the Bakerloo, using stock borrowed from the Piccadilly and Central London lines. The joint stock intended for the Watford extension was eventually delivered in 1920, and although lettered LNWR and LER, it was owned two-thirds by the LNWR and one third by the London Electric Railway and bore the LNWR livery throughout its life on the Bakerloo service. The stock was built by the Metropolitan Carriage & Wagon Company at Wednesbury, embodying British Thomson-Houston power equipment. For its main line role, car floors were higher than the Underground standard and minuscule luggage racks were provided. The stock comprised 3 motor coaches, 12 control trailers and 24 ordinary trailers formed into four or six car trains.

Work resumed on the Camden Town junctions in May 1919 and was completed in 1922, enabling full electric services from Euston and Broad Street to commence from 10th July 1922. The Croxley Green branch was electrified on 30th October 1922, and the conductor rail was extended to Rickmansworth (Church Street) on 26th September 1927 over the other branch from Watford.

For the expansion of services in 1922, the 'Oerlikon' stock was reinforced by 109 more vehicles, together forming 75 three car sets and 3 spare motors. The 1920s saw a considerable increase in suburban traffic and much overcrowding on the Watford line. A temporary expedient was the operation of a mixed set on the Earl's Court service, formed of two spare 'Oerlikon' motor coaches enclosing two or three LNWR composite corridor coaches. The corridor connections on the 'Oerlikon' stock were later removed in the mid-1930s.

To cope with the additional traffic and to speed up station stops, the GEC compartment stock was introduced in 1927. This formed part of a joint order shared with the Liverpool area, London receiving 17 motor thirds from the Metropolitan Carriage & Wagon Company, 12 composite trailers from the Clayton Wagon Company, and 12 control trailer thirds by the Midland Railway Carriage & Wagon Company. The electrical equipment was provided by GEC to the Oerlikon design, and the new stock could run in multiple with the 'Oerlikon' sets. Motor coaches were powered by four 280hp motors and the three car sets could seat 40 first and 240 third class passengers. Ten third class trailers were constructed at Wolverton in 1929 in order to form some seven car trains. With the delivery of additional GEC stock in 1932, the fleet was increased to 25 three car sets plus 7 third class trailers which could be included within sets or coupled between sets to form seven car trains. When first class travel in the London suburban area was abolished from October 1941, seven car working ceased and the surplus trailers were stored — one had already been transferred to the Manchester to Altrincham line in 1939. The GEC stock was not allowed to work to Earl's Court, and had barred windows for the limited clearances in Hampstead Heath Tunnel on the North London line.

The joint tube stock with its manually-operated doors had a short life, and was replaced on the Bakerloo line during 1930/1 by standard Underground stock. Nine cars (three sets) were retained by the LMS, painted in its red livery and used on the two branch lines from Watford, causing less demand on the limited power supply to Rickmansworth than the full sized stock. They were taken out of service at the outbreak of war, and withdrawn officially in 1946.

The Willesden to Earl's Court service was withdrawn in October 1940 and the Siemens stock was stored until its eventual transformation for use on the 50 cycle Lancaster – Morecambe – Heysham electrification. The 'Oerlikon' fleet had suffered various losses due to accidents and enemy action, but systematic withdrawal commenced in 1957 as Eastleigh began to deliver the new Class 501 stock, and the last 'Oerlikon' set ran in revenue-earning service in April 1960. The GEC stock was never replaced — it was withdrawn, suddenly, during 1963 as a result of drastic train service reductions, both in frequency and length of trains. Some vehicles of both types lingered for a while in departmental service.

Plate 128 (below): A train of 'Oerlikon'-equipped stock of 1915-23 vintage approaches Euston on 5th May 1956 with a local service from Watford Junction. These sets had their accommodation in open layout form with passenger access via large doors at the vehicle ends.

J. N. Faulkner

Plate 129 (right): This splendid illustration shows a train of 1927 compartment stock introduced for London Division d.c. operation. The three car unit, with its driving trailer vehicle nearest the camera, is painted in LMS lined maroon livery. Note the second class number applied to each compartment door, identifying that the middle vehicle is of the trailer composite type.

Author's Collection

Plate 130 (left): All London Division d.c. stock was maintained at either Croxley Green or Stonebridge Park, from where they operated on both the Euston to Watford and Broad Street to Richmond routes. Departing from Brondesbury Park Station, a six car formation of 'Oerlikon' stock heads for Richmond during the early 1950s.

Author's Collection

Plate 131 (right): With a splendid array of semaphore signals, and an interesting notice on the left advising drivers not to exceed 35m.p.h. through the junction, a six car 'Oerlikon' train passes Acton Wells Junction with a Broad Street to Richmond service, again during the 1950s.

R. C. Riley

Plate 132 (left): A three car formation of 1927-32 stock, with its distinctive pointed rainwater strips on the coach roofs, slowly departs from South Kenton on 25th August 1953 with an 'all stations' service from Watford Junction to Euston. In this view, the driving trailer vehicle is nearest to the camera.

British Rail

Manchester to Altrincham Stock

The Manchester South Junction & Altrincham Railway (MSJ&AR) was a busy 8½ mile line serving the south-western suburbs of Manchester. Originally jointly owned by the London & North Western and the Manchester, Sheffield & Lincolnshire companies, the Grouping brought it under both the LMS and the LNER. When electrification was proposed in the 1920s, it was the LMS which led the project, and following the Pringle and Weir reports this was the first time the new British standard 1,500 volt d.c. overhead system was adopted.

Electric services commenced on 11th May 1931, with a basic 20 minute service and a total of over 80 trains per day. With ten intermediate stops, the journey time averaged 23 minutes, cutting several minutes off the previous steam schedules. Services were operated by 24 three car sets, each formed of a motor coach, trailer, and a driving trailer of compartment type stock, seating 228 third and 40 first class passengers. The carriage design was similar to stock built by the LMS for its London and Liverpool electric lines a few years earlier. Livery was the dark green of the MSJ&AR's stock.

The steel-framed and panelled coaches were built by Metro-Cammell with electrical equipment supplied by GEC on the 'Oerlikon' system. Each motor coach was powered by four 328hp motors, giving a maximum speed of 70m.p.h., and current collection was by means of a pantograph. When six car trains were run during peak hours, the two sets were formed with their motor coaches at the outer ends. Some down-grading of first class accommodation took place in the post-war years.

The 1,500 volt traction was cut back from Manchester (London Road) to Manchester (Oxford Road) from 14th September 1958, to enable the route to be converted to 25kv a.c. supply as part of the Manchester to Crewe electrification project. The d.c. trains then terminated in the bay platforms at Oxford Road. By 1970, they were some of the oldest stock running on the mainland for BR, and it was decided to convert the MSJ&AR to 25kv operation so as to integrate its services with those towards Crewe. The last day of d.c. operation was 30th April 1971, and a.c. traction started on 3rd May. Some of the trailer coaches have found homes with preservation societies, but the majority of vehicles were scrapped.

Plate 133 (below): The first application of 1,500 volt d.c. overhead came in 1931 with the MSJ&A electrification between Manchester (London Road) and Altrincham. The same stock, albeit with many detail differences, remained in operation until the route was re-equipped at 25kV a.c. in 1971. A morning Altrincham to Manchester commuter train enters Brooklands Station, in this view, formed of 2 three car units.

Martin Welch

Section D : NE/BR (ER) Third Rail

Tyneside Electrics

The first electrification by a British main line railway was accomplished almost simultaneously by the Lancashire & Yorkshire and the North Eastern railways. The NER adopted the third rail 600 volt d.c. system for its electrification of the North Tyneside suburban lines. The first section from Newcastle (New Bridge Street) to Benton was inaugurated on 29th March 1904 and, in stages, electric traction was extended to the coast at Tynemouth and back to Newcastle, both via Wallsend and via the Riverside branch. The final conversion, on 25th July 1904, involved a stretch of the East Coast Main Line between Heaton and Benton Quarry, and shortened the journey for residential expresses from Newcastle to the coast. A short link between Manors and New Bridge Street was opened on 1st January 1909, and this completed the circular route to the coast. The system had a route mileage of 37, and the 20.6 miles of the circular route was scheduled to take 63 minutes.

The main contractors were British Thomson-Houston (BTH), and only sixteen months elapsed between signing and the public inauguration. British Thomson-Houston and Westinghouse provided equipment for 100 multiple unit coaches of saloon pattern with clerestory roofs to be built at the NER's York Works. Each motor coach was powered by two 125hp General Electric motors. An attractive red and cream livery distinguished the electric stock from the normal NER crimson lake applied to conventional locomotive-hauled stock.

Initially, 48 of the vehicles were single cab motor coaches, 8 were double cab motor coaches, 5 were double cab driving trailers, 12 were single cab driving trailers, and 27 were ordinary trailers. About half the motor coaches had luggage compartments, and most of these were first class but were soon altered to composites. The number of double-ended motor coaches and control trailers was increased by conversions in 1905. The standard train was a three car unit, but considerable variety in formation was possible.

In addition to the passenger vehicles, there were two motor parcels vans which were used at each end of the 6-wheel coaches, on morning and evening workmen's trains. Another parcels van was added in 1908 and, from 1909-15, passenger stock was reinforced by eleven motor coaches and eleven trailers, latterly to cope with increased wartime traffic to the nearby shipyards.

Disaster struck on 11th August 1918 when a fire at the Walker Gate car shed destroyed 34 coaches and damaged others, so that a partial reversion to steam traction was necessary. It was not until 1920 that replacement stock emerged from York Works; the 34 vehicles were similar in layout to the originals and took their old numbers, but differed in appearance by having elliptical roofs and had slightly more powerful 140hp motors. Another replacement motor coach was built in 1928 following the loss of a 1904 car in a collision. A fourth motor parcels van was added to stock in 1921.

The arrival, in 1937, of the Metro-Cammell articulated stock caused the withdrawal of the surviving 1904-15 vehicles. The 1920 replacement stock was, however, found suitable to operate the new electric service to South Shields, which was opened on 14th March 1938. The existing motors were still usable and the coaches were completely refurbished and

repainted. The provision of bucket seats reduced the seating capacity slightly, but the second driving cabs were removed and three motor coaches were converted to trailers. A new motor coach with luggage compartment was built at York to make up the total to 36 vehicles, to operate as 18 two car sets.

In its turn, the refurbished 1920 stock was displayed by the Eastleigh-built two car sets in 1955, and the last NER stock ran to South Shields on 17th May 1955. However, three of the trailers had been converted by BR to permabulator vans, and these lingered for a few more years coupled to the Metro-Cammell stock to cater for the family outings to the coast at summer weekends.

The LNER's replacement of the original NER stock took the form of 64 articulated two car sets by Metro-Cammell, each powered by two 216hp Crompton Parkinson motors. The coaches had steel frames and bodies with open saloons, and manually-operated sliding doors at each end. The livery was a revival of the NER red and cream, and this also replaced the LNER varnished teak on the refurbished 1920 stock. From 1941, the livery was changed to blue and off-white — perhaps anticipating British Rail's corporate image!

The articulated twin sets (112ft. 7in. overall) came in four versions; 12 units formed motor third with control trailer third, 16 units formed luggage motor third with control trailer first, 18 units formed motor third with trailer third, and finally, 18 units with luggage motor third and trailer first. The trailer first could be converted to composite for off-peak traffic. Trains could comprise two to eight cars in any combination of units.

In addition to the sets there were two single cars — luggage motor thirds, with cabs at each end. These were intended to work with the workmen's train, now formed of six NER bogie compartment coaches. This train having fallen into disuse, these cars were downgraded to perambulator vans, spare parcels vans or towing units. To replace the three original NER parcels vans, two new Metro-Cammell vans were built in 1938.

BR Replacement Stock

The BR replacement stock for the Tyneside electric network came in 1955 when Eastleigh Works produced 15 two car sets of almost identical design to the Southern Region's 2EPB units, except that larger luggage vans were provided. Each two coach unit was formed of a Motor Brake Second Open (MBSO) and a Trailer Second Open (TSO), the total passenger loading being 176, front end indication being given by marker lights and a central route indicator. After the decision was taken to de-electrify the route from 1963, the sets were transferred to the SR and converted into conventional EPB sets, but retained their larger luggage vans.

The high cost of electricity supply and declining traffic levels on Tyneside led to the adoption of a policy of replacing electric traction by diesel multiple units. The South Shields line was the first to go, on 6th January 1963, and the Eastleigh two car sets moved to their native region. The North Tyneside system was slowly run down and electric working finally ceased on 17th June 1967 when all the LNER stock was withdrawn.

Plate 134 (right): The first stock for the North Eastern Railway (NER) Tyneside electrification looked very American in appearance, having clerestory roofs and end doors. The total stock for the original NER scheme was 39 motor and 33 trailer vehicles. A three car set is illustrated here. Noteworthy on this stock is the match-boarded lower body sides, more normally associated with Pullman car stock.

Author's Collection

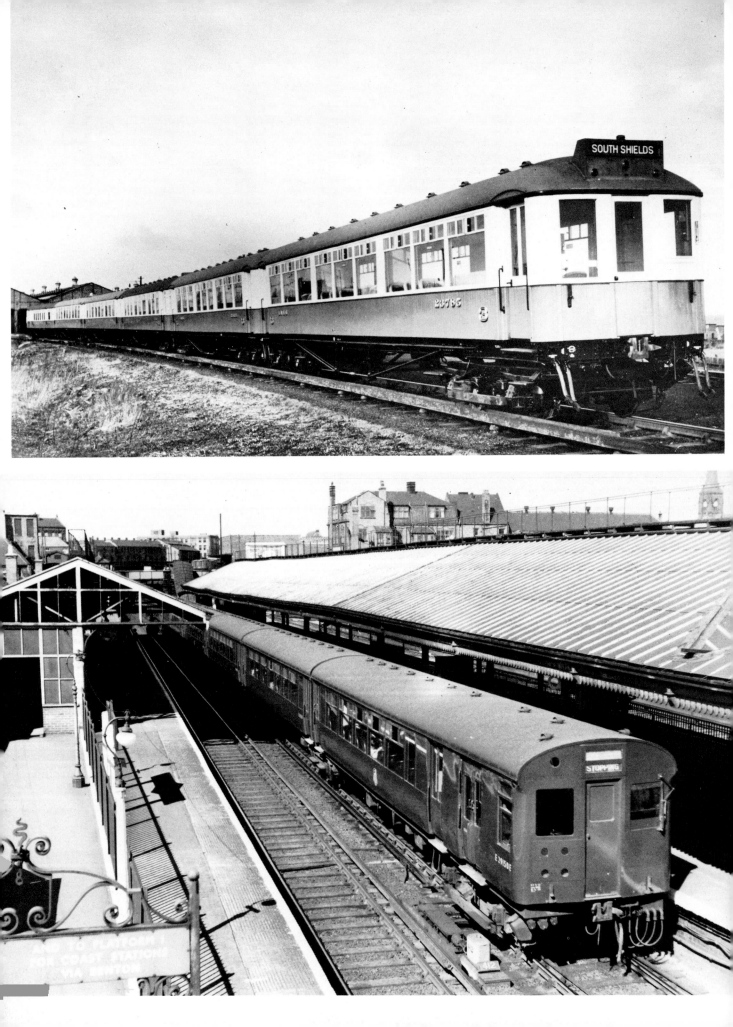

Plate 135 (above left): During 1920/1, additional stock emerged for use on the North Tyneside routes, being displaced in the 1930s by articulated two car sets, the 1920/1 stock then going via the carriage shops to emerge in 1938 for use on the South Tyneside routes to South Shields. A six car formation, led by driving third car No. 23785, is seen at South Gosforth Depot early in 1938.

British Rail

Plate 136 (below left): The 1937 replacement stock for the Tyneside lines was constructed by Metropolitan-Cammell, and consisted mainly of two car articulated sets. On 15th August 1959, 3 two car 'Artic' sets stand at Manors with a Tynemouth to Newcastle, via Benton, service.

John Faulkner

Plate 137 (above): On a murky 4th March 1964, a four coach train, formed of two 'Artic' sets, arrives at Percy Main Station with a North Tyne Loop diagram. One unusual feature of this stock was the fitting of sanding equipment in case of adhesion problems; a very rare fitting for electric unit stock.

Colin Boocock

Plate 138 (below): During 1938, two purpose-built parcels vans were introduced, replacing original 1904-8 vintage vehicles, each car being fitted with full driving controls at each end and four sets of double-leaf sliding doors on each side. No. E29467 stands at Manors with a Tynemouth to Newcastle working on 15th August 1959.

John Faulkner

Plate 139 (above left): The 1920/1 stock remained in service on the South Tyneside route until 1955, when the railway works at Eastleigh produced a fleet of two car electro-pneumatic brake-fitted units as replacements, closely resembling SR EPB units of the period. A two car unit, with car No. E77108 leading, is seen outside Eastleigh Carriage Works during February 1955, just after completion.

Les Elsey

Plate 140 (below left): Although the new SR-built Tyneside stock was of EPB appearance, major differences included the fitting of a destination indicator and route panel in the upper part of the front end, and the position between the two front windows was taken by four white and one central red rear marker lights. On 16th September 1962, the 10.23 South Shields to Newcastle train arrives at Tyne Dock Station.

Ian S. Carr

Plate 141 (above): On grounds of economy, the Tyneside electric network was de-electrified in 1962 with the services being replaced by diesel multiple unit formations. On 15th August 1959, the 10.00 Newcastle to South Shields train makes ready to depart from Newcastle (Central) Station and is formed of two Eastleigh-built Tyneside units.

John Faulkner

Plate 142 (below): One single motor luggage van, No. E68000, was also constructed at Eastleigh in 1955 for Tyneside operation, being of almost identical appearance to the SR motor luggage vans of the period. The car had four double-opening doors on each side, and was capable of carrying 3 tons of luggage at each end.

British Rail

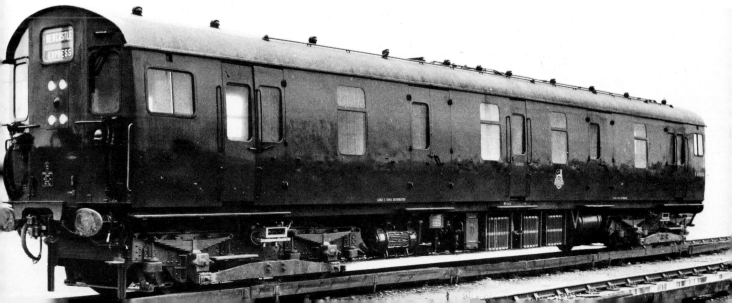

Section E : GE, GN/BR (ER) — Overhead

Class 302

During 1958, the first of 112 four coach units for the Tilbury line emerged from the BR workshops at York and Doncaster. Each four coach set was formed of a Driving Trailer Second (DTS), Motor Brake Second (MBS), Trailer Composite (TC) and a DTS. Passenger accommodation was provided in the high density style, with each unit providing seats for 19 first and 344 second class passengers.

Technical equipment was supplied by English Electric, four traction motors of 190hp each being carried one on each axle of the MBS vehicle. Mercury arc rectifiers were provided to convert the 6.25/25kV a.c. into d.c. for traction. Conventional equipment on the unit ends consisted of a buck-eye coupling and buffers at draw gear height, with air and control jumpers on the nose end.

By the end of 1960, all the 112-strong fleet was in service, although it was actually constructed before being needed for the Tilbury line, thus enabling it to be used on other routes while older stock was receiving conversion from d.c. It has been reported that at least two units temporarily operated in the Manchester area, and also one unit in the Glasgow electrified complex. These were presumably test or proving runs and it is not known whether the units were actually in revenue-earning service.

The allocated number series of these units was 201-312, and this has been prefixed by the class number in recent years.

When the final unit emerged, it was fitted with a silicon rectifier and a Brentford transformer to give stepless control. Many tests were undertaken with the unit on various sections of line and, in 1964, it entered Wolverton Works for further modifications, this time having thyristor control equipment fitted. Again, a thorough testing programme was carried out and, by 1972, the experiments were deemed completed, and so the unit passed through works and emerged with standard equipment.

On introduction, units were painted in BR multiple unit green, changing in the 1970s to BR rail blue, and subsequently to Inter-City blue and grey. In common with a number of Eastern Region electric multiple unit types, a refurbishing programme has been carried out during the early 1980s. These sets have passed through BREL Eastleigh and Wolverton works and work has included the opening out of all vehicles, applying the latest upholstery and generally improving the environmental conditions, together with the refurbishment of technical equipment, and alterations to coach layouts to give the formation of DTC, MBS, TS, DTS which we see today.

Plate 143 (below): Classified by BR as Class 302 are these 112 four coach Tilbury line units. The set illustrated, No. 205, is painted in multiple unit green livery with yellow lettering, and is operating a test special during the early 1960s. When constructed, these units carried just two headcode numbers between the front windows; however, soon after their introduction, 4-digit identification numbers were decided upon.

Author's Collection

Plate 144 (above): When the final Class 302, No. 312, emerged, it was something of a test bed, fitted with a silicon rectifier and Brentford transformer, thus providing stepless control. From 1964, the unit was again modified and fitted with thyristor control equipment. No. 312, painted in multiple unit green livery, is seen on the Tilbury line during 1965.

GEC Traction Ltd.

Plate 145 (below): In common with the majority of electric multiple units, various liveries have been carried. This illustration of set No. 246 displays the short-lived all-over blue colours with the small yellow warning panel. The set was photographed at Barking, on 23rd December 1967, while on a Fenchurch Street to Shoeburyness working.

John Faulkner

Class 305

Class 305/1

The 52 three car units of Class 305/1 were built by BR at York Works from 1960, to operate suburban services from Liverpool Street to Chingford and Enfield Town. The prime recognition feature is the configuration of the seating, which is arranged entirely in second class open saloons. Each unit has a total capacity for 272 persons.

Traction is derived from the four 200hp traction motors which, like the ancillary equipment, are GEC-designed and manufactured. At first, they were fitted with liquid-cooled mercury arc rectifiers, but these have subsequently been replaced by silicon rectifiers.

The units are carried on rather dated-looking double bolster type bogies, incorporating 'knife edge' suspension. The power car has the guard's accommodation incorporated within, and thus has less passenger accommodation. Units are currently running in the formation; Driving Trailer Second (DTS), Motor Brake Second (MBS) and DTS, each car being sub-divided into two passenger saloons, the seating of which is arranged in bays, the power cars having eight bays and the trailers nine. Each bay has its own passenger door of the slam type.

During 1984, a start was made on withdrawing some of the older members of the class, while others have been reformed into four car units, incorporating redundant trailer vehicles from other units.

Class 305/2

These units are almost identical to their Class 305/1 sisters, in terms of electrical equipment and control gear, but were built as four car sets, the additional vehicle being a Trailer Composite (TC), seating 19 first and 60 second class passengers. Intended for service on the lines at Bishop's Stortford and Hertford East, they were constructed by BR Doncaster Works on York-fabricated frames. The majority of the class was introduced in 1960, and in the intervening quarter of a century has seen service on most of the Great Eastern electrified network. At the time of writing, the entire class was allocated to Ilford, but over the years, Clacton Depot has also had an allocation.

When built, both Class 305/1 and Class 305/2 units sported a four character alpha-numerical route indicator box above the driver's windows at roof height. They ran with these in situ for many years after BR decreed that the route indicators were not necessary, following the introduction of modern computerised signalling systems. More recently, the redundant boxes have been modified to display two marker lights in a black surround, similar to certain locomotive classes.

All Class 305/2 units have been refurbished in recent years to enable them to conform to modern standards of passenger comfort. This work has included the addition of plastic-based internal trim, to discourage graffiti, and the use of flourescent strip lighting. Alterations have again been made to set formations, and the fleet now operates in the formation DTC, MBS, TSO and DTS.

Plate 146 (below): Of the two types of Class 305 unit in service, designated 305/1 and 305/2, recognition of the two types is comparatively easy as the 305/1 units are three coach sets, whereas the 305/2 type are four coach formations. Of typical early 1960 electric multiple unit appearance, Class 305/1 No. 409, introduced for the Liverpool Street – Chingford – Enfield Town line, is shown in pristine condition on 11th May 1960, soon after delivery.

British Rail

Plate 147 (above): Class 305/1 No. 430, with its pantograph stretching high into the sky, runs into Northumberland Park Station on 19th March 1983 with the 15.09 Hertford East to Liverpool Street train. The stilt-mounted GE signal box at this location adds considerable interest to the view.

Michael J. Collins

Plate 148 (left): The four car Class 305/2 units, numbered in the 501-519 range, were introduced for GE outer suburban operation with increased seating capacity. Painted in green livery with a small yellow warning panel, unit No. 519 departs from Broxbourne on 5th October 1963 with a Bishop's Stortford to Liverpool Street working, while BTH Class 15 locomotive No. D8210 makes ready to depart with a vans train from the station yard.

John Faulkner

Plate 149 (right): During the early 1960s, various high visibility warning panels were applied to some GE stock of Classes 305 and 306. Sets emerged with full height yellow panels between the two cab windows, giving a very strange appearance to the stock. Set No. 508 approaches Bethnal Green with a Liverpool Street to Bishop's Stortford working.

John Faulkner

Class 306

Electrification work on the Great Eastern system began prior to World War II, but the section from Liverpool Street through to Shenfield was not completed until September 1949. Subsequently, extensions to Chelmsford, reached in June 1956, and Southend (Victoria), reached in December 1956, were undertaken using the same 1,500 volt d.c. overhead system.

The 92 three car Class 306 units were constructed to fulfil these services and were arranged in a Driving Motor Brake Second (DMBS), Trailer Second Open (TSO), Driving Trailer Second Open (DTSO) formation. The Birmingham Railway Carriage & Wagon Company (BRCW) furnished the major part of the order, but the DTS vehicles were manufactured by Metropolitan Cammell, the power/control equipment being supplied by English Electric.

The power car was marshalled at one end and was 60ft. long, some 5ft. longer than the trailer cars, the total unit length being 170ft. Power was collected by a diamond-shaped pantograph on the roof of the DMBS, the actual roof level being lowered to make room for this equipment. Under the pantograph, the guard's compartment was incorporated. Traction equipment was provided by four 210hp traction motors under the DMBS car. When new, units were fitted with headlight type route indicator codes, similar in design to those employed on the Manchester to Glossop/Hadfield stock on which these units were based. In addition, a roller blind destination indicator, for passenger identification of service, was provided.

During 1960, the GE electrified network was converted to a.c. operation and the Class 306 units were converted to this system, and an amount of original equipment was still usable with the addition of a new transformer and rectifier. All additional equipment was housed in the intermediate trailer, which was rebuilt to accommodate the standard Stone-Faiveley pantograph and the guard's compartment. These units were carried on Thompson-designed bogies for their entire life, and were restricted to 75m.p.h.

At first, the stock carried no unit numbers, reliance being placed on the individual carriage numbers for identification. Later, in the mid-1950s, trains were allocated set numbers which were carried on discs which were clipped on to the front. The original numbers were in the series 01-92, and the third digit of '0' was added as a prefix when the units were rebuilt. Unit numbers were then painted on.

Unit No. 030 was withdrawn in late 1968 as a result of a serious fire, but the class as a whole was not considered to be life-expired until the late 1970s. Replacement commenced as the more up to date Class 315 sets were introduced on GE lines from 1980. Throughout their lives the class stuck fairly rigidly to the Liverpool Street – Shenfield – Chelmsford/Southend (Victoria) routes, making only occasional forays beyond. During the late 1970s, however, one unit was diagrammed occasionally to work as far east as Colchester, on winter Sundays.

After withdrawal, units were stored at a number of locations, some lingering for over a year at March East Yard before being despatched to breakers' yards in the Midlands and the North. A lucky few have survived, but only in departmental service at Ilford, and are now mainly in an unrecognisable state.

Plate 150 (below): The pioneer electric scheme of the Eastern Region GE section came into force in 1949 with the electrification of the Liverpool Street to Shenfield line at 1,500 volt d.c. overhead. The stock provided was in fixed three car formations, with tall pantographs mounted on the roof of the motor coaches. Carrying a unit target disc, No. 46, a three car set, is seen at Ilford during the early 1950s.

Author's Collection

Plate 151 (above): This side view of a three coach set displays the stock in 'as built' condition, each coach having two pairs of double-leaf sliding doors on either side, which were operated by passengers under the supervision of the guard.

Author's Collection

Plate 152 (below): A side elevation detail view of an original design trailer second car for the 1,500 volt GE sets. When the units were rebuilt for a.c. operation, one end of the trailer second car was replaced by guard's van, and a pantograph was mounted on the roof.

Author's Collection

Plate 153 (left): With the pantograph at probably its lowest operating level prior to passing under a road bridge a three car set, led by the motor vehicle, stands at Chadwell Heath in September 1949, soon after public service was introduced. A strong resemblance exists between these units and the Class 506 sets used in the Manchester area, to which these sets served as prototypes.

Author's Collection

Plate 156 (right): From their introduction in 1949 until their demise in the early 1980s, the Class 306 sets have always been allocated to the sizeable electric multiple unit depot at Ilford, where anything from seat cleaning to major body repairs could be undertaken. Two Class 306 units, a 302 unit and three Class 305 sets, stand in the carriage cleaning shed at Ilford during 1970.

GEC Traction Ltd

Plate 154 (right): During the late 1950s, it was decided to use a.c. power supply for the remaining GE electrification, and the 1,500 volt d.c. sections were therefore re-equipped for a.c. operation. The stock also needed to be rebuilt, and this work included major structural alterations involving the removal of the pantograph and brake compartment from the driving motor car to the intermediate trailer. Other alterations included the fitting of a two position headcode and the applying of unit numbers. Three car a.c. fitted No. 062 leads a nine car formation past Stratford, on 8th July 1961, with the 12.25 Liverpool Street to Southend service.

John Faulkner

Plate 157 (right): The final end for the Class 306 units came in the early 1980s, following the introduction of 1972-designed Class 315 units. Set No. 023 passes Bethnal Green, on 3rd November 1980, with a Liverpool Street to Gidea Park duty. After conversion of the units to a.c. operation, the two driving cars looked alike, however, the motor coach was still identifiable by the omission of control jumpers on the nose end, these only being carried on the driving trailer vehicles.

Colin J. Marsden

Plate 155 (left): A number of units were rebuilt some months prior to the d.c. system being abolished, and thus operated on the 1,500 volt system with the power collection being afforded from the trailer vehicle. With a vertical yellow warning panel, a nine car set (operating on d.c.) passes Romford, on 25th June 1960, with a Gidea Park to Liverpool Street working.

John Faulkner

Class 307

When the line to Southend (Victoria) was electrified at 1500 volt d.c., 32 four car units were built by BR at Eastleigh Works on frames manufactured at Ashford. Subsequently known as Class 307, they were given three figure unit numbers from the start. At first, however, they were given an 'S' prefix to distinguish them from other electric stock. The electrical equipment housed in the units was supplied by GEC; traction being derived from four 174hp motors, mounted two on each bogie on the motor second coach.

The class, as delivered, was similar in outward appearance to the Class 302 and had the same centrally-placed roller destination blinds at cant rail level, and the same type of lamp route indicators. The alphanumerical route indicator boxes, situated between the driver's windows, were a later modification. Presently running in the formation Driving Trailer Brake Second (DTBS), Motor Second Open (MSO), Trailer Second Open (TSO), and Driving Trailer Composite (DTC), this stock has the distinction of being the first four car electric unit designed by BR aimed specifically at medium distance work. The internal layout, therefore, formed the basis of several subsequent BR designs.

In 1960, the class was converted to a.c. operation with much original equipment being reused, but the opportunity was taken to fit germanium rectifiers which give better performance. The guard's accommodation and pantograph was resited in one of the driving trailer vehicles during modification work, and the units were reformed, retaining their former seating capacity of 362 persons.

Today, most of the units are mounted on BR-designed Mk. II bogies, but unit No. 307.111 has been experimentally fitted with B4 style bogies in an attempt to improve riding at speed. It is understood that the experiment has been successful, and several more units will be similarly treated as bogies become available from redundant locomotive-hauled stock.

Like many of the Eastern Region formations, this class must run as a minimum of two cars to complete the electrical circuit from overhead wire to traction motors, but the facility does exist for the TSO to be omitted from a formation if required. In practice, however, this rarely happens. The class are equipped to run in multiple with other ER units, except those of the latest genre, but are most frequently seen working with Class 308 units to which they are internally similar.

The class has worked from Ilford Depot for most of their lives with only temporary and relatively short-lived sojourns at Clacton Depot. They were numbered 01-32 in the original scheme, but renumbered 101-132 upon conversion for a.c. operation. More recently, under the TOPS classification scheme, sets have become numbered 307.101-307.132.

Plate 159 (above): By the late 1950s, conversion work was underway on the stock to enable operation from the then standard a.c. power system. The conversion work was major, and included the repositioning of the pantograph and guard's van from an intermediate to a driving vehicle. Rebuilding and subsequent overhauls were undertaken at Eastleigh for a number of years, and it was while unit No. 122 was returning to the ER from Eastleigh, that this photograph was taken of the set stabled at Surbiton on 16th April 1965.

John Faulkner

Plate 158 (left): The Shenfield to Southend (Victoria) line was also electrified at 1,500 volt d.c., and stock for this route was constructed at Eastleigh Works. To distinguish this stock from others operating on the GE section, an 'S' suffix was applied to unit numbers. In this 1957 illustration, 2 four car sets are seen in 'as built' condition. Note the large d.c. power jumper cable on the unit end.

Author's Collection

Plate 160 (right): The appearance of the Shenfield Class 307 units has gone almost full circle, as, when first introduced, no route indicators were carried. These were subsequently installed from the early 1960s, but have again been removed as sets were refurbished during the 1980s. Other alterations have included the fitting of sealed beam headlights and major seating amendments. Set No. 307121 approaches Shenfield, on 8th January 1983, with the 09.45 Southend to Liverpool Street service.

Kim Fulbrook

Class 308

Class 308/1

Constructed during 1960/1 at York, nine of these units, Nos. 133-141, were introduced for use on the then newly-electrified Colchester to Clacton line. A further 24 sets, Nos. 142-165, were commissioned for operation out of Liverpool Street on outer suburban duties. The whole class was built to operate from 25kV a.c. from new. The Clacton to Colchester line was intended to be a test bed for this new standard of electrification. Internally identical to the Class 307 sets, the new units sported a modified front end arrangement built to a more 'up to date' profile. Gone was the slab front end of the previous design, to be replaced by a front end which sloped inward from waist level. A roller destination blind was fitted between the driver's windows, and the four aspect alpha-numerical route indicator was resited to a new position, being centrally-mounted at roof level above the front windows.

The units were fitted with English Electric equipment, and the 154 ton sets were carried on Gresley-style bogies and powered by four 200hp traction motors. The formation of sets were: Battery Driving Trailer Second (BDTS), Motor Brake Second (MBS), Trailer Composite (TC), and Driving Trailer Second (DTS) and, like most of the older GE units, have a maximum speed of 75m.p.h. Since 1981, these units have been undergoing a refurbishment programme to equip them for continued service into the 1990s, and in an attempt to curb increasing on-train vandalism. This work has entailed an internal refit, stripping out old fittings and replacing them with up to date materials. This has included fluorescent lighting, new seats and converting compartment stock to open layout vehicles. In addition, vandal proof plastic-based trim has been fitted to the internal carriage walls. The new formations are DTC, MBS, TS and DTS.

Class 308/2 and 308/4

This build comprised nine extra units destined for use on the LTS section, which were identical to the main build except that the power car was a motor luggage van (MLV) and not for passenger use. The intention was to use them for late evening or early morning trains when passenger demands would be low and passenger accommodation could, therefore, be sacrificed in favour of parcels and mail.

Service conditions later proved that this was impracticable because unit diagrams sometimes required the use of these sets on peak hour trains, and the loss of 96 seats led to unpleasant overcrowding and, as a result, four of the cars were rebuilt in 1971, at Wolverton Works to the MBSO vehicles. These units containing the converted vehicles form the sub-class 308/4, and they remain on the LTS section based at East Ham Depot. They now bear the numbers 308.313-308.315.

The remaining five units were allocated Class 308/2 and Nos. 318-321, and were a familiar sight at Shoeburyness on Fenchurch Street off-peak workings for some years. In peak times, one or two sets would be stabled in sidings at Tilbury (Riverside). They ran in the formation DTS, MLV, DTS, and were latterly renumbered to Nos. 308.991-308.995. In 1984, one of the DTS vehicles in each set had its seats removed for additional luggage space and was reclassified DTLV

More recently, the changed nature of BR traffic demands, and a decline of interest in the parcels business, has made the units surplus to Eastern Region requirements, and thus they face the ignomy of withdrawal in the near future.

Plate 161 (below): The Class 308 units, currently divided into three sub- classes, are of standard 1960 electric multiple unit style, and are to be found on both the Liverpool Street and Fenchurch Street sections. In 1961, 9 four car sets were introduced, which incorporated a full length Motor Luggage Van (MLV). Unit No. 317, complete with luggage van, is illustrated.

Author's Collection

Plate 162 (above): Class 308/1 units are numbered in the 133-165 range and are utilised on GE outer suburban services, being allocated to Clacton and Ilford depots. On 6th May 1978, Class 308/1 unit No. 156 leads Class 307 unit No. 112 on the 10.32 Liverpool Street to Southend (Victoria) train, and is photographed at Harold Wood.

Brian Morrison

Plate 163 (below): A number of alterations have been carried out on the Class 308 fleet over the years. The original four coach units that incorporated MLVs have seen the greatest change; four sets had the luggage vans rebuilt into passenger stock during 1971, and the remainder are now operating as three car sets and have been renumbered. Set No. 308994 arrives at Pitsea, on 3rd August 1983, leading the 17.17 Fenchurch Street to Shoeburyness train.

Brian Morrison

Class 309

Constructed by BR York Works, the 76 cars which form Class 309 were introduced to services on the Liverpool Street to Clacton line from January 1963. The fitting of Commonwealth bogies enabled them to operate at speeds up to 100m.p.h., and they were viewed as prototypes for new standard express electric multiple unit stock. In fact, however, this never materialised. When new, the Class 309 units were decked out in an all-over maroon livery, the only BR electric multiple unit to carry this scheme, but they now run in the standard BR blue/grey Inter-City colours with full yellow warning ends; a livery which they received from 1968.

Originally, they were divided into three sub-classes; eight two car sets (309/1), eight four car sets with griddle cars (309/2) and finally seven four car sets without catering vehicle (309/3). The latter have the formation: Driving Trailer Composite (DTC), Motor Brake Second (MBS), Trailer Second Open (TSO), and DTC. Based on the Mk. I coach design, these units featured a novel seating arrangement, as second class accommodation was provided in either open or compartment cars.

The main electrical equipment was supplied by GEC, with Brown-Boveri circuit breakers and Stone Faiveley pantographs. For many years the four 280hp motors installed in each unit made them the most powerful electric multiple unit on BR; this distinction only being surpassed by the Southern Region 4REP sets.

The 166 ton units remained in their original formation for about eight years, but in 1972 changes began to occur. The griddle car from No. 616 was withdrawn, due to a frame defect, and was replaced by a converted diesel multiple unit trailer buffet, No. W59831, built by Swindon in 1964. This vehicle became the only item of Class 309 stock to run on BR Mk. IV bogies. In 1974, two car sets Nos. 605-608 were strengthened to four car sets by the addition of former locomotive-hauled Mk. I SK and CK stock,

rebuilt by BREL Wolverton for its electric multiple unit career.

The wrap-round driver's windows of the units was a notable feature when new, but these proved to be costly to replace in the event of mishaps, and in 1975 modifications were instituted, replacing the original windows with a pair of flat panes of laminated glass, separated by a corner post.

In 1980, 'Travellers' Fare' decided to withdraw catering facilities from the line, and the griddle cars were gradually taken out of service. These were replaced by converted CK vehicles from units Nos. 605-608, thus converting them to three car sets. Meanwhile, the remaining two car sets, Nos. 601-604, were strengthened by the addition of a converted locomotive-hauled coach to each set, thus making these into three car sets.

The Class 309 units have been very restricted in terms of route worked, and they have always been rare off their native Clacton to Liverpool Street route. During 1976, set No. 604 worked on the London Midland Region, when it was involved in a series of high speed trials on the West Coast Main Line to evaluate equipment at high speed.

For the future, the East Anglia electrification gives the class a new lease of life, and a refurbishment programme was instigated at Wolverton Works in 1984. The sets will emerge rebuilt to modern standards, and the remaining three car units will be strengthened to four car formations with the addition of a converted locomotive-hauled vehicle.

It has been reported that British Rail intends to use the units on boat train services to and from Harwich, and possibly on Ipswich line services as well as their usual Clacton duties, when the new electrification is complete.

Plate 165 (above): Over the years, many unit reformations have taken place within the ranks of Class 309. This has included reforming the two car sets into three car formations, removing the buffet vehicles from some four coach sets, and rebuilding some locomotive-hauled vehicles into electric multiple unit standards to augment sets. An eight car formation with unit No. 309616 leading (complete with buffet car) approaches Colchester during 1979 bound for Liverpool Street.

Michael J. Collins

Plate 164 (left): For the new electrified 'express' service between Liverpool Street and Clacton/Walton, a sizeable fleet of Class 309 corridor units was introduced formed into various two to four car formations. Painted in its distinctive maroon livery with yellow central door, a two car unit, No. 604, stands at Clacton-on-Sea soon after delivery in 1962.

Author's Collection

Plate 166 (right): Operating as a three car set after the removal of the buffet car, a formation of Class 309 stock nears Chelmsford in June 1983, led by set No. 603. It will be noted that the cab windows have been amended if this and the first illustration of this section are compared, the new flat glass screens being fitted in the course of economy.

Michael J. Collins

Class 312

Between 1975 and 1978, a fleet of main line or outer suburban units for LMR and ER operation was built by BREL at York, based on the successful LMR Class 310 build of the mid-1960s. The fleet, running to 49 units, can be divided into three main types — Nos. 312201-4, allocated to the LMR for Birmingham area operation; Nos. 312701-26, allocated to Hornsey for GN outer suburban duties; and Nos. 312781-99 which are housed at Clacton and used on GE outer suburban diagrams.

The unit and vehicle design closely follows the Class 310, but a gangway is provided throughout each four car unit, which is formed of a Driving Trailer Second (DTS), Motor Brake Second (MBS), Trailer Second (TS) and a Driving Trailer Composite (DTC). All vehicles are set out for high-density occupation (3 + 2) and a four coach unit has accommodation for 25 first and 297 second class passengers.

Although these units were introduced as late as the mid-1970s, an age when the four character route indicator was almost a thing of the past, this equipment was fitted in the same style as on Class 310 units. In recent years, the alpha-numerical blinds have been replaced by a black screen, with two white cut-outs acting as marker lights. One detail difference between these and the Class 310 build is in the driver's nose-end windows. On Class 310 units, wrap-round glass was provided in both the driver's and assistant's windows, but following a number of costly replacements it was decided to use flat frontal screens with a corner post.

Power collection is provided by a roof-mounted pantograph above the guard's van on the MBS vehicle, and all traction/control equipment was supplied by GEC, being mounted in underframe pannier boxes. For traction, four GEC 270hp traction motors are installed, two on each bogie. One unusual feature of a modern electric multiple unit is the provision of voltage changeover equipment (25kV-6.25kV), on Nos. 312781-99, this being necessary for their operation on the Great Eastern section, which takes them on to sections where 6.25kV a.c. is still in use. The four units allocated to the London Midland Region are restricted to 75m.p.h., whereas the Eastern Region sets have a maximum speed of 90m.p.h. The lower restriction is imposed as the Class 310s, which they operate alongside, are limited to the lower speed.

When constructed, the sets were painted in the all-over rail blue livery, this soon being changed to the rail blue/grey we see today. These sets are scheduled to remain in operation well into the next century.

Plate 167 (below): The most modern of ER main line electric multiple units are the Class 312 sets, which are based on the LMR Class 310 units of the mid-1960s. The Class 312 units are allocated to both the GE and GN sections. Set No. 312001 stands inside Hornsey maintenance depot, in May 1976, with two Matterson lifting jacks being positioned. This set is now numbered 312701.

British Rail

Plate 168 (above): As well as building the Class 312 units for the ER, four additional main line electrical multiple units, classified as 312/2, were built for LMR operation in the Birmingham area. These Class 312 units are almost identical to the Class 310 sets, except that different windows and a revised style of nose end grab handles are fitted.

British Rail

Plate 169 (right): Class 312 units allocated to the GN section of the Eastern Region are maintained at Hornsey, and are usually used on King's Cross to Royston duties. On 22nd March 1982, Class 312 No. 312721 emerges from Welwyn North Tunnel with the 14.55 Royston to King's Cross train.

Brian Morrison

Class 313

Designed in 1972, this class was the first of a long line of similar units (*see Classes 314, 315, 507 and 508*), which were based on the experimental high density PEP prototype of the early 1970s. The three car variant, introduced in 1976, was designated Class 313 and featured the ability to collect power from the 25kV a.c. overhead of the King's Cross suburban electrification, and from the 750 volt d.c. third rail in the tunnel section from Drayton Park to Moorgate. The build ran to 64 units, comprising 192 individual cars which were all constructed at BREL, York Works.

The 103 ton units run in Driving Motor Second (DMS), Trailer Second (TS) and DMS formation, and are powered by eight 110hp GEC traction motors, four under each DMS vehicle. Each set has a total seating capacity of 232 second class passengers, and units can be coupled by means of 'Tightlock' couplers to form six car sets in peak periods, providing accommodation for 464 seated and over 200 standing passengers. Maximum unit speed is 75mph, when working from the 25kV system, but this is reduced to only 30mph on the short d.c. section.

Both DMS vehicles have an integrated driving cab and guard's compartment at the outer ends, with 74 seats arranged 'back to back' in the 2 + 3 configuration with a central gangway. The interior trim panels are designed for easy removal in the event of repair or possible future refurbishment, and melamine finish is used for the bodyside waist panel, ceiling, cross partition. end partition and end doors.

Passenger entry is via air-operated twin sliding doors — two on each side of each car. The seat shells are individually-mounted and pre-formed in glass reinforced polyester and are fitted together to form the double or treble seat layout. Removable covers and detachable seat back cushions facilitate easy cleaning and maintenance. A 'Ripper' communication system is provided between driving cabs for the train crew, and the equipment can also be used as a public address system.

Braking is accomplished through rheostatic and air-operated disc brakes, actuated from a single driver's brake controller using the 'Westcode' system. Control circuits are arranged to give bias to the electric brake system, thus increasing disc pad life. Automatic reversion to air braking takes place at speeds too low for effective rheostatic braking. Trip cocks are fitted to facilitate automatic braking in the tunnel sections, if required.

The overall length of a three car unit is 198ft. 4in. The sleek external finish of the train is enhanced by the application of the BR two-tone blue/grey livery, with full yellow ends sporting a stylish 'wrap-round' on to the body side. A narrow orange band at cant rail height marks the safety line for staff working on the stock beneath energised wires.

Originally, the entire class was allocated to Hornsey electric multiple unit depot, but they have seen use outside the Great Northern system. A few were used on the St. Pancras to Bedford line for crew training prior to delivery of purpose-built Class 317 units, and to cover stock shortages when the line was commissioned. Others have seen service on the Great Eastern Clacton to Colchester section (with trip cocks and rheostatic brakes removed) to cover stock shortages pending refurbishment of some older units. From May 1985 the sets commenced operation on the Euston to Watford d.c. lines, replacing life-expired Class 501 units.

Plate 171 (above): When introduced, all Class 313 units were allocated to Hornsey for GN operation. However, from the early 1980s, a shuffle of rolling stock took a few members of the class to Clacton for GE service, and from 1983 some units were placed on long term loan to the LMR for 'Bed-Pan' duties to cover shortages of Class 317 sets. No. 313001 slowly passes through the washing machine at Hornsey in April 1976.

British Rail

Plate 170 (left): The first 'fleet' derivative of the 1972 design high density stock was the Class 313, designed for GN suburban services from Moorgate/King's Cross to Welwyn Garden City. Arriving at Wood Green, on 3rd June 1979, a six car formation, led by unit No. 313055, forms a Welwyn Garden City to Moorgate train.

Brian Morrison

Plate 172 (right): Until its closure at the end of 1983, BREL Horwich Works was responsible for major repairs to Class 313 sets. After Horwich Works closed, York Works became the main overhaul point. Two units, Nos. 313045 and 313042, stand side by side in Horwich Works yard in 1981, and one unit appears to have suffered serious collision damage.

Colin J. Marsden

Class 315

Intended for the intensely-worked Liverpool Street to Shenfield inner suburban services on the Great Eastern section, the Class 315 unit is a four car variant of the successful 1972 design high density stock. Control gear, appearance, and general layout are broadly similar to the Class 313 introduced from 1976 on the Great Northern lines. The Class 315 units commenced operation in 1980, and filled the role previously undertaken by the older Class 306 units. Formation of sets being Driving Motor Second (DMS), Trailer Second (TS), TS and DMS, the units have a total seating capacity for 318 second class passengers, first class accommodation not being provided.

Power is collected from the overhead catenary by a roof-mounted single arm pantograph on one of the TS vehicles, and associated electrical equipment is mounted in boxes underslung between the bogies. Although introduced as late as 1980, it is surprising to observe that these sets were fitted with four character alpha-numerical route indicators, displayed above the route learner's window. More recently, this feature has been blanked off, following technical improvements in signalling techniques. The destination blinds, mounted above the right-hand driver's window, however, are still used for passenger information.

Some 86 units have been supplied, but it is interesting to note that 19 have GEC equipment/traction motors in place of Brush-manufactured equipment installed in the remainder. This was carried out as part of British Rail's new purchasing strategy, designed to decrease reliance on one manufacturer and to spread orders through a variety of suppliers. The corollary, of course, is that unnecessary expense is generated through the need to carry two sets of spare parts at depots and main works.

All units are allocated to Ilford Depot and, for some time, when new, operated as far east as Southend (Victoria). Complaints from passenger organisations about lack of toilet facilities for such a lengthy journey precipitated a rethink of stock policy, and the units were, from spring 1984, restricted to inner suburban services, which meant that British Rail was able to diversify some of the workings. This led to the appearance of Class 315 units on the Chingford lines and in North-East Essex as far as Bishop's Stortford. Like their Class 313 sisters, these units also saw some operation on the Bedford to St. Pancras/Moorgate electrified line during its commissioning in 1983-4.

Grimsby & Immingham Tramway

The Great Central Railway, in 1912, completed its new port on a green field site at Immingham on the south bank of the River Humber. The labour force was mainly drawn from the Grimsby area, and a temporary rail motor service was succeeded by a cross-country electric tramway, a rare British example of a practise familiar on the Continent. The first section from Corporation Bridge in Grimsby Docks to a point called, optimistically, Immingham Town, was opened on 15th May 1912. After a reversal there, an extension inaugurated on 17th November 1913 carried the line to the Immingham Dock terminus, at the end of the east jetty. The stub end at Immingham Town was extended to Queen's Road to serve the village, but completion in 1915 was not followed by any regular service.

The town section in Grimsby, as far as Cleveland Bridge, was a single track street tramway with passing loops and a 12m.p.h. speed restriction. The Pyewipe car sheds were situated here at the start of the country section. The single track electric tramway, with its passing loops, ran parallel to the freight line from Grimsby to Immingham. Along this stretch, the limit was 25m.p.h. and with few inhabitants here to use the request stops, progress was usually rapid. The final extension from Immingham Town to the Dock was double track, alongside the dock road.

The complete seven mile run took about 25 minutes and a basic half-hourly service was provided, but at shift times convoys of cars would follow each other closely. Power supply was 500 volt d.c. with the usual tramway overhead wiring.

The standard design of car was a long bogie vehicle with 64 seats and two trolley poles, built by Brush and powered by two 50hp motors. Four were supplied in 1912, four more in 1913 and a final batch of four in 1915. In addition, there were four smaller cars with 35hp motors and 40 seats, built by Brush in 1912 for an authorised extension of the tramway into Grimsby town centre, which was never carried out. These cars saw little service, and one was converted into a works car while the others were withdrawn.

Industrial development on Humberside increased traffic during the years after World War II, and British Railways took the opportunity of tramway abandonment on Tyneside to obtain additional single deck cars. Three veteran cars were purchased from Newcastle Corporation in 1948, built by Hurst Nelson in 1901. These had 40 seats and took the numbers 6-8 vacated by the original short cars. The ex-GCR cars were numbered 1-4 and 9-16, and this series was followed by 17 cars (Nos. 17-33) obtained from the Gateshead & District Tramway Company, in 1951. These 48-seater bogie cars were the newest in the fleet, having been built by Brush and the Gateshead company between 1921 and 1928. British Railways replaced the Tyneside liveries and the LNER teak or brown with the green shade used for its electric trains.

As the trams were blamed for traffic congestion in Grimsby, on 30th June 1956 the street section beyond Cleveland Bridge was closed; tram passengers then had to transfer to a Corporation bus to complete their journey. This inconvenience, increasing car ownership, and the age of the tramway fleet, combined to cause the total withdrawal of services from 1st July 1961. Fortunately GCR car No. 14 and ex-Gateshead car No. 26 have been preserved by the Tramway Museum Society.

Plate 174 (left): Although this book does not set out to illustrate the electric tramway systems of Britain, one small system, operated by the Great Central Railway and under BR from 1948, has been included. Ex-Great Central Railway car No. 16 is shown at Cleveland Bridge on 18th October 1960. The livery applied to this car was similar to SR electric multiple unit green, and has yellow numbering and lettering.

Colin Boocock

Plate 175 (below): Such was industrial development on Humberside that in post-war years additional cars were required. Some were acquired from Newcastle Corporation but the largest number (16 vehicles) came from the Gateshead & District Tramway system. A 48 seater ex-Gateshead Tramway car, No. 26, is seen at Immingham Dock in this 1960 view.

Colin Boocock

Plate 173 (left): The body style for the 1972-designed electric multiple unit was adapted into no less than five different production fleets, and the final derivative was the Class 315, for GE operation. GEC-powered unit No. 315855 approaches Romford, on 2nd September 1981, with a Liverpool Street to Gidea Park service.

Brian Morrison

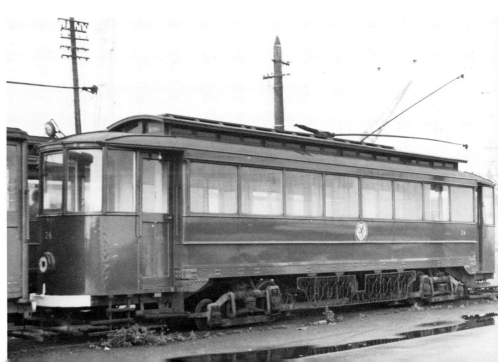

Section F : ScR — Overhead
Classes 303 and 311

Class 303

A total of 91 three car sets was introduced between 1959 and 1961 for the Glasgow suburban electrification scheme. These 91 sets, which were later to become Class 303, were ordered in two separate fleets of 35 and 56 units, and were constructed by Pressed Steel Ltd. The units were laid out for all second class occupation in the high density mode of (3 + 2), with passenger access being by two pairs of double-leaf air-operated sliding doors on each side of each vehicle. Unit formations were: Driving Trailer Second (DTS), Motor Brake Second (MBS) and DTS; the total loading for a three car unit being 236, but of course, with the provision of sliding doors, somewhat roomy vestibules are available which can increase the loading of a unit to around 350 by standing passengers. Power and control equipment is supplied by AEI (Metropolitan Vickers) and is carried in and underneath the MBS vehicle. Four 210hp traction motors are provided and all vehicles are mounted on Gresley-type double bolster bogies, braking being provided by automatic air and electro-pneumatic equipment, the maximum unit speed being 75m.p.h.

In common with a number of Eastern Region electric multiple units of the period, the Class 303s were dual-voltage sets, as both 6.25 and 25kV equipment was fitted. One departure from previous electric multiple unit tradition, and considered at the time to be of considerable advance, was the provision of a glass partition between the passenger saloons and the driver's vestibule/cab, enabling passengers to observe the route ahead. Front end equipment on these sets consisted of a destination indicator above cant rail height, and a two position numerical indicator (now dispensed with) under the central cab window, multiple unit control jumpers and air pipes being provided under the window. When connected, this equipment allowed up to three units to be controlled by one driver. A centre buck-eye coupler with rubbing plate was also provided as were side buffers. When introduced, a livery similar to Caledonian blue was applied but, over the years, this has been superseded by BR rail blue, followed by BR blue/grey, and from 1984, a number of units emerged in Greater Glasgow (GG) orange and black livery. Set numbers allocated are 001-091, which in recent years have been class-prefixed to give the six figure TOPS number.

From the late 1970s, several Class 303 units were reallocated to the London Midland Region for operation in the Liverpool to Crewe area, being allocated to Crewe Electric Depot. This was the first departure from Scotland since the class was introduced.

Class 311

In 1967, additional stock was required mainly for extension of lines on the south bank of the Clyde. This was provided by 19 almost identical units built by Cravens, with power and control equipment supplied by AEI. The internal layout of these sets, which became Class 311, was the same as on the Class 303 units, except for the modern decor applied and fluorescent lighting fitted.

Class 311 units usually operate alongside the Class 303s, and from the outside, recognition can be difficult. Unit numbers allocated to Class 311 are 092-110, which are now class-prefixed.

From 1984, the Class 303/311 fleet have been passing through BREL Glasgow Works for a heavy overhaul, which has been locally deemed as 'life extension'. This work included cosmetic attention, basically improving the passenger environment. However, some frontal alterations have also been made, including the plating over of the former headcode box and the installation of two headlights.

Plate 176 (below): The Glasgow suburban units, introduced from 1959 and built by Pressed Steel Ltd., became affectionately known as the 'Glasgow Blue Trains' by local inhabitants and staff alike, and this was because, when introduced, they were painted in a striking mid-blue or 'electric blue' livery. Sporting no unit number, a three car set poses for an official photograph soon after introduction.

British Rail

Plate 177 (above): Originally it was only the routes north of the Clyde that were electrified and, following this scheme, passenger returns rose considerably, and frequently trains arrived at Glasgow full, and sometimes with standing passengers. On 8th September 1963, set No. 035 arrives at Westerton, the junction for Milngavie and Singer, with a Milngavie to Springburn working.

John Faulkner

Plate 178 (below): Following the 1967 South Clyde electrification, a further fleet of three car units was required. To fulfil this need, 19 identical sets to those already in use was constructed, but this time by Cravens Ltd., and were classified as 311. Class 311 unit No. 092 stands at Wemyss Bay on 20th January 1980 with the 12.20 service from Glasgow (Central).

Brian Morrison

Class 314

Sixteen 1972-designed high density units, classified as 314, were introduced in 1979 for Glasgow suburban operation. These three coach units follow the same external layout as Classes 313, 315, 507 and 508, and are formed of a Driving Motor Second (DMS), Trailer Second (TS), and a DMS, the DMS vehicles accommodating 68 second class passengers, with the intermediate trailer seating 76. Each unit is gangwayed within and has emergency end doors, mainly for tunnel operation, two pairs of double-leaf sliding doors being provided on both sides of each coach. The TS vehicle carries a roof-mounted pantograph of the single arm type, and between the bogies a considerable amount of technical equipment is located.

Traction/control equipment for the first six units was supplied by Brush in the form of eight TM6-53 traction motors, together with associated thyristor control equipment; while the remainder of the fleet is fitted with GEC type G310AZ traction motors and thyristor control equipment. All units are fitted with air-operated disc and rheostatic brakes. In common with all other 1972-designed units, automatic 'Tightlock' couplers are fitted which transmit both buffing and traction forces. Under the 'Tightlock' coupler is an electrical/air connection box together with a drum switch which is under the control of the driver for coupling/uncoupling.

Class 314 units are allocated to Hyndland Depot and, on introduction were painted in BR blue/grey livery. However, from early 1984, a start was made to outshop the stock in Greater Glasgow (GC) orange/black livery; a most striking colour scheme which well suits the stock.

Plate 179 (below): To augment the Class 303/311 units operating on the Clyde network, a fleet of sixteen 1972-designed high density units was introduced from 1979 and classified as 314. Unit No. 314212 stands at Dalmuir, on 27th August 1983, with the 12.44 to Motherwell, via Singer, and Glasgow (Central) low level.

Tom Noble

Plate 180 (above): The first six Class 314 units were constructed with Brush Traction equipment, whereas all subsequent sets incorporated established GEC equipment. The first GEC unit, No. 314207, awaits departure from Lanark, on 20th October 1983, with the 11.24 limited stop train for Glasgow.

Tom Noble

Plate 181 (below): During the autumn of 1983, BR and Strathclyde Passenger Transport Executive came to an agreement to have the suburban units of Classes 303, 311 and 314 outshopped in the PTE orange and black livery, in order to achieve a corporate image with the already orange-painted Glasgow buses and underground trains. The first unit so treated was Class 314 No. 314216, seen arriving at Motherwell on 22nd August 1983 with the 12.26 train from Dalmuir.

Tom Noble

Class 370 (APT) — Inter-City Development Train

Over the years, much has been said and written about the development of the Advanced Passenger Train (APT) concept, and it is not the intention of this volume to cover this subject again. After the gas turbine Advanced Passenger Train — Experimental (APT-E) had been tested, together with the sophisticated tilt principle, a fleet of six pre-production APT-P half trains was constructed. Each half train was formed of a Driving Trailer Second (DTS), Trailer Second (TS), Trailer Restaurant Second Buffet (TRSB), Trailer Unclassified (TU), Trailer First (TF), Trailer Brake First (TBF) and a Motor (M), providing seating for a total of 268 passengers. The technical equipment in the motor cars provided by ASEA is of the thyristor type, providing four times 750kW body-mounted traction motors.

thus provides a total train accommodation for 536. All vehicles in the train are fitted with a cant system, enabling the train to negotiate curves on the present BR tracks at a significantly higher speed. The external contours of the vehicles are basically the same as the gas turbine train, but considerable redesign work was undertaken on the front ends — the main reason being the requirement for the fitting of buffing and drawgear which, if the need arose, could be used to haul the train by a conventional locomotive. In addition to the fitting of the main electric power plant in the centre of a train formation, an auxiliary low-powered diesel engine is installed just behind the cab sections in DTS vehicles. The nine degree cant system, installed in the APT-E train, was heavily modified for fitting into the electric unit. It was decided not to fit the cant system in the same way on power cars, as the roof-mounted pantographs could not be permitted to move the nine degrees from vertical, or the train would be likely to de-wire. To overcome this problem, a complicated anit-tilt system was designed with direct linkage between the bogies and pantograph.

All vehicles for the APT project were constructed at Derby, the power cars assembled at the locomotive works and the trailer vehicles at the Litchurch Lane Works. Once suitable vehicles were completed in 1978, the two former Class 252 HST power cars, now in departmental service, were used to haul various APT cars around the network for testing pur-

poses. From early 1979, when there were enough APT cars available, the stock was transferred to Glasgow (Shields Road) Depot from where test on the West Coast Main Line took place. The maximum permitted speed for the train was usually 125m.p.h. but, on a number of occasions in connection with speed testing programmes, speeds of up to 160m.p.h were recorded.

Throughout 1980/1, the train operated timetabled specials where all equipment was placed under arduous test conditions, unfortunately failing on a number of occasions. The main problem areas involved the cant system, and considerable modification work was undertaken. In December 1981, the stock was put into public service, but such were the problems encountered that after only a couple of days, the stock was returned to Shields Road for more exhaustive testing and modifications. From 1982, the stock commenced working regular timetabled empty stock runs again from Glasgow, and usually to London on a daily basis. On more than one occasion the stock has been placed in semi-revenue earning service, conveying railway staff as 'guinea pigs' on the Glasgow to Euston run, to gauge public acceptance of the train and, in particular the tilt system, but on a number of trips even these runs had to be curtailed.

From 1984, less and less finance was placed into the APT project and it is now very unlikely that the train will ever enter public-timetabled service in its present form.

From the spring of 1984, the train was renamed from Advanced Passenger Train to the Inter-City Development Train (ICDT), and it is understood that numerous further experiments and development work will be necessary to the train — some are likely to include the conveyance of passengers. One major modification will include the alteration of some of the articulated vehicles by mounting them on conventional underframes.

From August 1984, it was again decided to introduce the Class 370 stock on selected Glasgow to Euston trains on two days per week, and on each run passengers were given a questionnaire regarding passenger comfort and services, in an effort to gain their reaction.

Plate 183: APT construction was undertaken by BREL Derby, power cars being assembled at the locomotive works, and passenger vehicles being built across the road at Litchurch Lane. This illustration shows a power car undergoing base painting at Derby Locomotive Works on 2nd September 1978.

Peter Gater

Plate 184 (below): Prior to the consideration of APT suitability for public service, exhaustive tests and evaluation running had to take place, which often led to short and unusual formations occurring. Here a six car train with two power cars nears Beattock, on 21st October 1983, with a high speed pantograph test special bound for Quintinshill. On this occasion, the train was specially authorised to travel at speeds of up to 155m.p.h.

Tom Noble

Plate 182 (left): The Inter-City Advanced Passenger Train made its first appearance on BR tracks in 1978, each unit being formed of seven coaches which made up half a train. With a driving trailer second nearest to the camera, part of a 'half-train' stands at the Railway Technical Centre, Derby, in 1979.

British Rail

PART 2 — D.C. ELECTRIC LOCOMOTIVES
Section A : SR/BR

Class 70

It was about the time of the outbreak of Word War II, in 1939, that the electrical engineer of the Southern Railway, Mr A. Raworth, obtained outlining permission to construct three straight electric locomotives, primarily for freight operation. After the initial plans were produced and submitted to the Southern Railway Board, objections were raised, principally from Mr O. V. S. Bulleid, who insisted that all projected main line locomotives must be of the mixed traffic type. After further negotiations, Mr Bulleid's case was accepted and the Southern's drawing office produced final plans for a Co-Co locomotive of very box-like appearance, with a full width driving cab at each end.

A major technical problem with the electric locomotive principle soon became apparent as with 'gaps' of larger than a locomotive length existed in the live rail, power would be lost from the locomotive. This could jolt the train, causing buffer locking, or even stall a train if speed/momentum was low. To overcome this problem, a 'booster' was planned; this was a flywheel-driven generator, enabling a proportion of power to be supplied by the momentum of the flywheel whilst traction power was lost. This 'booster' electric system would be sufficient to coast through gaps of 100ft. at a minimum speed of 12m.p.h. After plans had been accepted by the Southern Railway Board, construction commenced at Ashford Works, with the first machine, carrying Southern Railway number CC1, emerging in the autumn of 1941.

In addition to the locomotive having live rail pick-ups on each bogie, a diamond roof-mounted pantograph was provided for use in yards where the presence of a live rail would be dangerous to railway staff. The first of the 'booster' electrics was rated at 1,470hp, having a maximum rail horsepower of 2,200 at 35.5m.p.h. The second electric locomotive, numbered

CC2, emerged in 1943. It conformed to the same basic style as No. CC1, but incorporated a number of minor detail differences. The two pioneer electrics operated mainly on the Central Section, usually from Brighton on freight traffic to and from Redhill or Norwood. Problems were few and, in 1945, the reliability levels rose to over 80 per cent. The third of the locomotives sanctioned for construction in the early 1940s was not built until 1948, this time at the Brighton Workshops. Again, it broadly resembled the previous two machines but, if anything, was even more box-like in appearance, having a slab-fronted cab, very similar to the SUB electric stock of the period. As this locomotive did not make an appearance until after nationalisation, it carried the BR electric series number, 20003.

Although the three locomotives were constructed to mixed traffic requirements, their main work was on freight diagrams. However, following the gradual decline in freight traffic in the post-war years, other work was needed for the fleet, and this was found on the Victoria to Newhaven boat trains, where the locomotives gave sterling service. After the decline in the boat traffic, the machines saw less and less work but, for a number of years, were used to haul the Royal Train from Victoria to Tattenham Corner on Derby Day.

By the late 1960s, when the 'in' word with the British Railway Board was standardisation, the fleet was deemed as surplus. After spending a short period out of use at Brighton, all three were withdrawn in 1969 and sold for scrap.

Although these machines were not the most handsome ever constructed, they gave the railway some favourable service and provide a good test bed for BR's E5000 series machines.

Plate 186 (above right): When the second of the SR electric locomotives emerged in 1943, it was very similar to the first, but a number of improvements were included following experience with No. CC1. With its pantograph raised high, No. CC2 is seen painted in the SR green livery and carrying the 'Southern' slogan on its side, when new.

British Rail

Plate 185 (below): The first of three Southern Railway 'booster' Co-Co electric locomotives, No. CC1, appeared in the winter of 1941 and, after initial testing, took up trial running on the Brighton main line, making frequent visits to Brighton Works for adjustments. No. CC1 stands outside Brighton Works painted in lined grey primer.

Author's Collection

Plate 187 (below right): The third SR electric locomotive No. 20003 did not appear until after nationalisation, although when outshopped it was still in SR malachite green. From 1959 the BTC decided that all diesel, electric and gas turbine locomotives would be painted in a black and silver livery. No. 20003 appeared in the new 'modern traction' colours from March 1950 and is seen here on display at Waterloo on 22nd March.

British Rail

Plate 188 (above): From early 1945, No. CC1 appeared in Southern malachite green with the 'Southern' slogan midway up the body side. During 1945, No. CC1 worked alongside No. CC2, usually on freight traffic, between Norwood and Brighton. In this 10th October 1945 view, No. CC1 is seen departing from Norwood Yards with a 1,000 ton freight, bound for Redhill.

British Rail

Plate 189 (right): When constructed, No. CC1 was fitted with a 2-character headcode (stencil) position, but after only a short period, this was plated over and electric headlamps were fitted, with folding discs for daytime operation. In original condition, No. CC1 passes Merstham, on 5th December 1941, with one of its first test trains, returning to Brighton.

British Rail

Plate 190 (left): One of the regular duties for the SR original electric locomotives, later classified 70 by BR, was the Royal Train and, in particular, its yearly visit to Tattenham Corner, taking Her Majesty The Queen to Epsom Racecourse for the Derby meeting. Operating the Royal Special in 1968 was No. 20003, outshopped in rail blue livery with a full yellow end. It was photographed at Tattenham Corner shortly after arrival from Victoria.

John Scrace

Plate 191 (above): The 'booster' locomotives were usually associated with the Central Section, being allocated to Brighton Depot. On 20th May 1954, No. 20003 was entrusted with the job of hauling a lengthy train of Pullman cars from Victoria to Brighton, conveying railway dignitaries to the International Railway Congress. The train was captured on film passing Preston Park Pullman Works.

J. H. W. Kent

Plate 192 (below): Perhaps this class of locomotive will always be associated with the Victoria to Newhaven boat train duties which were in their hey-day during the 1940-1960 period. On 27th May 1949, No. 20002 nears Balham with a Victoria to Newhaven boat train, carrying passengers on the first leg of their journey to Paris.

Author's Collection

Plate 193 (above): Soon after introduction, No. 20003 was put to work alongside its sisters on main line freight duties between Brighton and Norwood. Apparently with its pantograph removed, No. 20003 passes Hayward's Heath, on 15th October 1948, bound for Norwood Junction.

British Rail

Plate 194 (left): Painted in black livery, with aluminium lining at waist level, No. 20003 passes Redhill, on 16th April 1955, with a Brighton-bound freight. During the 1960s, when all three machines passed through Eastleigh Works, a number of modifications were carried out, including the removal of the nose end air and jumper cables.

John Faulkner

Plate 195 (right): After machines passed through Eastleigh Works in the 1960s, the 'wind-up' headcode system was fitted, and all former nose lights removed. Although this cleaned up the front end, it gave an even more slab appearance than hitherto. No. 20003 passes through Wandsworth Common at the head of a Victoria to Newhaven boat train.

John Scrace

Class 71

Under the British Transport Commission (BTC) 1955 modernisation plan, the Kent Coast main lines were authorised for electrification. The majority of stock to be used was of electric multiple unit formation, but for express passenger/freight duties mainly to and from the Kent Coast sea terminals, a fleet of twenty four 2,552hp 'booster' electrics was ordered, classified by the SR as the E5000 or HA series and under the BR TOPS classification as 71.

These 'new' generation electric locomotives, mounted on a Bo-Bo wheel configuration, collected power either via third rail collector shoes or a roof-mounted pantograph, the latter used in yards where the presence of a live rail would not be acceptable for safety reasons. Although, at first glance, these locomotives seemed very similar to the Bulleid/Raworth design of the 1940s, a number of significant differences were incorporated. The 'booster' or flywheel was retained, but a total break from previous electric locomotive building was the provision of fully spring-borne traction motors, together with SLM flexible drives. The 24 electric locomotives were ordered from the Doncaster Workshops where all components, including the bogies, which were of Swiss design, were assembled.

The design weight for the locomotives was 77 tons and a maximum tractive effort of 43,000lb. at 25 per cent adhesion was directed. The first machine, carrying the number E5000 emerged from Doncaster Works in late 1958, and was hauled to the Southern Region at Ashford, from where extensive test, trial and staff training runs were undertaken. By the end of 1960, the final member of the fleet was delivered. All were painted in the distinctive BR green livery and several members sported a red band mid-way up the body side panels.

Another change from the original d.c. locomotives was the provision of electric train heating. This was installed in favour of steam boilers as the SR intended to replace this archaic heating system at an early opportunity. When introduced, locomotives had their electric train heat-ing jumper mounted on the nose-end bodywork, but this was subsequently repositioned on to the buffer beam, following problems when coupling/uncoupling of trains. Another interesting point worthy of special note is that after the entire fleet had been in traffic for over two years, the first member of the class, No. E5000, was renumbered E5024! After the fleet was placed into regular daily operation, it proved totally reliable, returning availability figures of between 85-90 per cent on a number of successive months.

Class 71 locomotives were always used on duties in the South Eastern Section, with passenger work usually confined to the 'Golden Arrow' and 'Night Ferry' services. However, freight activities were more widespread, operating Continental freights to and from the docks at Dover, and the London distribution terminal near Hither Green.

By the mid-1960s, a number of the locomotives were deemed as surplus to operating requirements following a general decline in freight traffic, although technically there was still plenty of life left in them. About the same time, the Southern Region was interested in a fleet of medium-powered electro-diesel locomotives to operate in conjunction with the recently electrified Waterloo to Bournemouth route. After lengthy negotiations between BR and English Electric, it was decided that ten Class 71 straight electrics could be rebuilt into dual-powered electro-diesels. (*see Class 74 section*). The remaining Class 71 locomotives continued operating the two titled expresses between Dover and Victoria, together with a variety of freight, and mundane duties.

In 1977, BR decided that diagrams performed by the fleet could just as easily be worked by the region's Class 33 and 73 fleets, and from December 1977, all Class 71s were withdrawn. For a lengthy period, the fleet lay dumped at Ashford, Hither Green and Stewarts Lane depots, all eventually being sold for scrap, except No. 71001 which was rebuilt by BREL Doncaster and emerged as No. E5001, and is now on display at the National Railway Museum, York.

Plate 196 (below): Following the decision to electrify the Kent Coast main lines under the 1955 modernisation plan, it was decided to construct 24 'booster' electric locomotives for London to Dover boat trains and express freight operations. Carrying the 'Golden Arrow' headboard, No. E5014 leads a lengthy train towards London, near St. Mary Cray, on 15th September 1966.

Author's Collection

Plate 197 (left): Both the 'Golden Arrow' and 'Night Ferry' services were always associated with this class of locomotive. Although, on paper, Ashford Depot was responsible for their upkeep, Stewarts Lane Depot usually kept the machines, which were used on the prestigious workings, in mint condition. This splendid night exposure shows No. E5018 at Victoria, on 21st May 1965, with the southbound 'Night Ferry'.
Author's Collection

Plate 198 (right): Like the three Southern-designed d.c. electric locomotives, the Bo-Bo locomotives, later classified 71, were fitted with pantographs for depot and yard operation where the presence of a third rail would be dangerous. Drawing its current from the ovehead power line, No. E5001 stands in sidings at Hither Green Continental Freight Depot during 1960.
British Rail

Plate 199 (below): In original condition, with electric train heating supply cable on the front end, large headcode numerals and red bodyside band, No. E5001 passes Shortlands Junction, in June 1959, with a short vans train from Dover to Bricklayers Arms. At this time, most trains operated by the E5000 class were used for driver training.
Author's Collection

Plate 203 (right): Illustrations of Class 71 locomotives working the 'Night Ferry' service are somewhat rare owing to their early arrival time in London — usually long before many railway photographers had risen! No. 71001 approaches St. Mary Cray on 26th August 1976 hauling a splendid array of continental stock, only a few months prior to the locomotives being taken off the service.

Brian Morrison

Plate 200 (left): Although all locomotives in this class were in traffic by the end of 1960, they did not take over from steam traction on the 'Golden Arrow' until 12th June 1961, when No. E5015 was diagrammed for the train, seen here passing Shorncliffe. Note the two gold arrows on the side of the locomotive and the British/French flags displayed on the front.

The late Derek Cross

Plate 201 (right): The 'Night Ferry' service, conveying conventional stock from Dover to Victoria, fell to electric haulage as early as June 1959 when the locomotives were only a few weeks old. Still in pristine condition, No. E5003 passes St. Mary Cray on 12th June 1959 with the 'up' working.

The late Derek Cross

Plate 202 (left): After the 'new' electric locomotives had taken over the South Eastern's two most prestigious services, much publicity was given about the new accelerated and improved services. Dozing under the splendid overall roof at Dover, No. E5015 awaits departure with the 'up' 'Golden Arrow' on 13th October 1961. This locomotive was later rebuilt as a Class 74 electro-diesel and numbered E6101.

British Rail

Plate 204 (right): Displaying 'HA' in its headcode box — the SR designation for the Class, No. 71003 stands dumped at Stewarts Lane Depot on 6th February 1978. In the immediate period following condemnation, it was hoped to find other work for the fleet, but unfortunately this was not so. Except for preserved No. 71001, all were sold for scrap, some going to private scrap dealers while others were dismantled at BREL, Doncaster.

Colin J. Marsden

Section B : LNER/BR

ES1 (26500/1)

The 1904 North Tyneside electrification included the one mile freight branch from Trafalgar Yard, Manors, to the Quayside Yard, 130ft. lower on the banks of the river. The line dropped at a gradient of 1 in 27 through cuttings and a single line tunnel on a sharp curve, so that conditions under steam operation were appalling. Third rail electric supply was imperative in the narrow tunnel, but overhead wiring was necessary in the shunting yards.

For this difficult task, the North Eastern Railway (NER) built two Bo-Bo electric locomotives, Nos. 1 and 2, later becoming London & North Eastern Railway (LNER) Nos. 6480/1 and BR Nos. 26500/1. They were equipped with four 160hp British Thomson-Houston traction motors and Brush bogies, and at first they carried a bow collector on the bonnet, but this was later replaced by a pantograph on top of the steeple cab.

Trains were propelled downhill and hauled uphill with a maximum load of 160 tons. At the start of the ascent, it was the responsibility of the second man (or fireman) to switch in the collector shoes and to switch off and lower the pantograph, all within a few yards of dual supply at the entrance to the tunnel.

Among the loads hauled were the steam 0-6-0T tank engines en route between Heaton Shed and the riverside yards. The advent of the diesel shunter made electric traction unnecessary, and the branch was de-electrified from 29th February 1964, the two electric locomotives being withdrawn in September 1964. Fortunately, No. 26500 was preserved and is now at the National Railway Museum, York, as NER No. 1. The quayside branch closed from 16th June 1969, and its route is now crossed by the tunnel of the Tyne & Wear Metro.

Plate 205 (below): The 1 mile freight only branch from Trafalgar Yard, Manors, to the Quayside Yard was electrified in 1904, and two NER Bo-Bo locomotives were provided, power collection being effected either by slipper shoes mounted on each corner of the locomotive, or by a bow collector fitted to the bonnet at the No. 1 end. In original 'as built' condition, No. 2 is illustrated painted in NER green livery.

Author's Collection

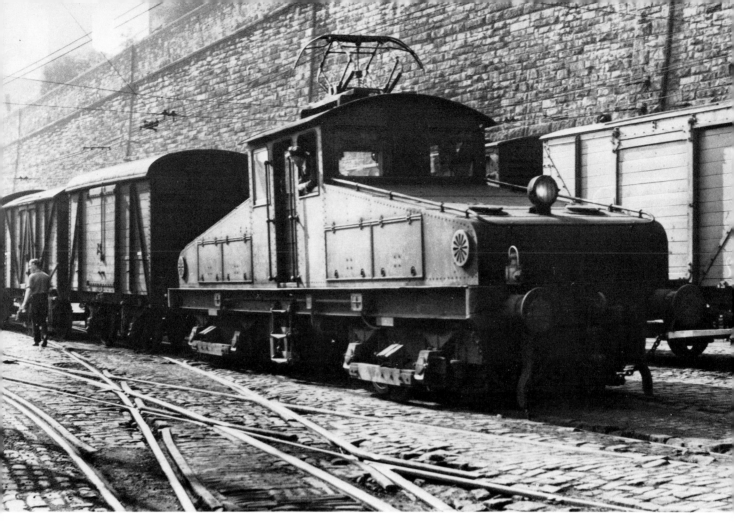

Plate 206 (above): After only a short period of operation propelling/hauling short freight trains up and down the 1 in 27 gradient, the bonnet bow collectors were replaced by the more conventional roof-mounted pantograph. No. 26500, formerly NER No. 1, shunts in Quayside Yard on 11th August 1953.

John Faulkner

Plate 207 (below): The two locomotives classified by BR as ES1 were allocated to Heaton Depot, alongside the electric unit stock used on the Newcastle area passenger network. Following the withdrawal of both ES1 machines in September 1964, they lay dumped at Heaton Depot until 1966, when No. 26500 was selected for preservation, and regretfully No. 26501 was sold to T. W. Ward at Choppington for scrap.

Derek Porter

EB1 (26502-11)

The North Eastern Railway (NER) handled a considerable amount of coal traffic from the Shildon and Bishop Auckland area mines to the docks and ironworks at Middlesbrough. The company felt, in the prosperous years before 1914, that this traffic justified electrification, and it embarked on one of the first examples of 1,500 volt d.c. overhead supply. The first section from Middridge Sidings, Shildon, to Bowesfield Junction was operative from 1st July 1915, and the full 18½ route miles from Shildon Yard to Newport East was completed on 1st January 1916.

Motive power was provided by ten 1,100hp Bo-Bo locomotives, built at the North Eastern Railway's Darlington Works, under the design of Sir Vincent Raven, with equipment being supplied by Siemens. They had centre cabs on which were mounted two pantographs. Originally numbered 3-12, they became LNER Nos. 6490-9 in 1946 and nominally BR Nos. 26502-11 from 1948. Their maximum load was 1,400 tons, and the 15 miles, mostly downhill, from Middridge Junction to Erimus Yard, Newport, took 57 minutes.

The inter-war decline of the coal industry made electric working uneconomic and the route was discontinued from 8th July 1935. The ten electric locomotives were put into store, firstly at Darlington and later at Gosforth. It was first envisaged that they might be used as banking engines on the Manchester – Sheffield – Wath electrification, but this was not to be. In 1949, No. 26510 was rebuilt and emerged with a single pantograph, and altered technical equipment increasing power for the machine to 1,256hp, and was moved to Ilford Depot on the Great Eastern section as depot shunter. One of the few outings for the machine was on braking trials between Ilford and Shenfield, during 1950, in connection with the MSW electrification. Final plans for this did not require the special banking locomotives, and the unrebuilt members of the class were withdrawn from August 1950. No. 26510 was transferred to departmental stock as No. DS100 in 1959, being finally withdrawn during 1963.

The design of this class formed the basis for the first batches of 1,500 volt d.c. locomotives for the Midi Railway of France, for which Dick, Kerr & Co. of Preston supplied the traction equipment in 1923.

Plate 208 (below): One of the most adventurous projects undertaken by the NER was the 1,500 volt d.c. electrification of the Newport to Shildon route. The locomotives were of a centre cab Bo-Bo design and had two pantographs. They were painted in NER livery with the distinctive NER crest on the cab door. NER No. 3 poses for its official photograph during 1914, some eleven months before construction of the line was completed.
Author's Collection

Plate 209 (right): Electric operation of the 15 mile Newport to Shildon route commenced from 1915, and continued for just twenty years before being de-electrified following the general decline in traffic over the route. NER No. 11 hauls a long and heavy coal train at Simpasture in May 1923, while en route for Shildon.

British Rail

Plate 210 (below): After the cessation of electric operation, the ten locomotives were placed in store at Darlington and Gosforth, with the hope that they would find other duties at a later date. In 1949, NER No. 11 was taken to Darlington Works and rebuilt with one pantograph and different technical equipment, before being transferred to Ilford on the GE section as a depot pilot and test locomotive for the 1,500 volt d.c. system then being introduced. After rebuilding, GNR No. 11 became BR No. 26510, and is seen at Ilford in October 1949.

C. C. B. Herbert

EE1 (26600)

At the end of its existence, the North Eastern Railway (NER) considered a project for electrification of its York to Newcastle main line. In 1922, Sir Vincent Raven built a prototype express locomotive, a massive 102 ton 2-Co-2 of 1,800hp, with a maximum speed of 90m.p.h. Electrical equipment was provided by Metro-Vickers, and the locomotive was fitted with dual brake equipment and a steam heat boiler. The machine was given the number 13.

NER No. 13 carried out some dynamometer car trials with a 460 ton train on the Shildon to Newport line, the only source of 1,500 volt d.c. in the country. It made a 'towed' appearance at the 1925 Stockton & Darlington Centenary celebrations, but otherwise spent its time stored at Darlington Works. The LNER had no money for electrification schemes, therefore the locomotive remained out of use. It was renumbered 6999 in 1946, and became BR No. 26600, being withdrawn along with the other Newport to Shildon locomotives in August 1950.

Plate 211 (below): In 1922, it was the intention of the NER to seek powers to electrify the York to Newcastle main line, using the 1,500 volt d.c. system. In anticipation of this, the works at Darlington built this large 2-Co-2 1,800hp twin-pantographed locomotive. Regrettably the scheme did not come to fruition, and the locomotive operated only a very few test trips on the Newport to Shildon line, eventually being scrapped in 1950.
Author's Collection

EM1, Class 76

The arduous route between Sheffield and Manchester, via Woodhead which, prior to the 1923 Grouping, was part of the Great Central Railway (GCR), was considered for electrification in the early 1920s but, for various reasons, this was not carried out. Proposals were again drawn up in 1926 just after the line had been taken over by the LNER, but regretfully these again were turned down. Some ten years on, the LNER, who had by then some operating experience of electric traction, drew up detailed proposals for a revised scheme, taking electric traction from Manchester (London Road) to Sheffield (Victoria), and on the branch from Penistone to Wath, and onwards from Sheffield to Rotherwood. The Railway Board and the Government approved the scheme and, by 1939, work commenced on the erection of track equipment — from the east end of the line. Regrettably, the outbreak of world hostilities in 1939 meant the suspension of the scheme but, about the same time, the LNER works at Doncaster commenced construction of a probable locomotive for the route. This was a Bo-Bo machine, designed by Gresley, and incorporated electrical equipment supplied by Metropolitan Vickers and the LNER, and was numbered 6701.

It was the LNER's original intention to make use of the redundant Newport to Shildon Bo-Bo locomotives now in store, and supplement these by new purpose-built mixed traffic locomotives. However, as time came to prove, this was not to be. After No. 6701 was completed, there was no suitable LNER electrified track on which to test it, and so in 1941 it was hauled across the Pennines to Manchester and used for a brief period on the Manchester South Junction and Altrincham (MSJ&A) route.

After the end of World War II, the LNER was not in an immediate position to recommence electrification work, and to complicate matters even more, a decision was made to make a second bore for the Woodhead Tunnel. In the meantime, the prototype locomotive, No. 6701, which had been renumbered 6000, was laying idle. The LNER were keen to test the machine in operational conditions, and agreement was reached between the LNER and the Netherlands Railway (NS) to operate the locomotive on their 1,500 volt network. Although the machine operated satisfactorily, the riding qualities were disappointing, particularly at speeds of between 45-60m.p.h. Such were the problems with No. 6000 that the LNER had a major rethink on the Manchester to Sheffield line motive power policy, which included a decision against using the stored Newport to Shildon locomotives.

Eventually, it was decided to construct 57 Bo-Bo machines of similar appearance to No. 6000 for lower speed mixed traffic duties, in addition to a fleet of Co-Co express passenger machines (*see next section*). The LNER prototype was returned to England in the late 1940s, where it was renumbered into BR stock as 26000, later being given the name *Tommy*,

a nickname applied to the locomotive by the Dutch Railway staff. Building of the production locomotives was awarded to the LNER works at Gorton, near Manchester, with power and control equipment supplied by Metropolitan Vickers. A number of detail alterations existed between the prototype and production locomotives, including cab window and door layout, and bogie fittings. Under the classification system of the post-1948 period, the locomotives were classified EM1. When the initial machines had been completed, the line was not ready for use and therefore several locomotives went into store, some on the GE section until the Pennine route was finished.

The electric service commenced from 4th February 1952, between Wath and Dunford Bridge with the sections between Manchester (London Road) and Dunford Bridge opening from June 1954, and the remainder of the line from Penistone to Sheffield during the following September. When introduced, the Bo-Bo locomotives were finished in BTC black livery, which subsequently changed to green and, of course, from the late 1960s, to standard BR rail blue. After introduction, the Bo-Bo mixed traffic locomotives operated jointly with the large Co-Co machines on passenger duties, as well as being in charge of numerous freight services. When built, the locomotives were fitted with air and electric regenerative brakes with vacuum for the train, however with the introduction of different stock and the need for a change in braking equipment during the late 1960s and 1970s, a number of machines received dual brake equipment, and some even acquired air brake equipment only. Another significant change within the fleet came in the late 1960s, when multiple control equipment was fitted to a number of locomotives, enabling up to three machines to be controlled by one driver, this system being especially useful with the introduction of long/heavy air-braked freight services. When the final twelve Bo-Bo locomotives were built, they were fitted with steam heat boilers and carried names associated with Greek mythology, as too did the Co-Co locomotives.

The Class 76 locomotives proved to be good reliable runners and even after passenger services were withdrawn, and the Co-Cos were sold, they remained in operation hauling lengthy freight trains, until BR decided that it was uneconomic to continue keeping the route and motive power operational. After much protest from public and staff alike, the line closed from 20th July 1981, with the equipment being removed (except for the section at the Manchester end which was retained for the Glossop/Hadfield services until 1984).

One locomotive, No. E26020, has been preserved and is now on display at the National Railway Museum, York, painted in its original black livery. All other members have been scrapped, some at BR premises but the majority by private scrap dealers.

Plate 212 (below):   The frames for what was effectively to become the prototype Class 76 locomotive were laid at Doncaster Works in December 1940, with the completed locomotive emerging in mid-1941. As the Woodhead route was incomplete when the locomotive carrying the number 6701 was ready for service, it operated a number of test trips on the MSJ&A 1,500 volt line. This illustration shows No. 6701, painted in the LNER lined green livery, in Doncaster Works during January 1941.

British Rail

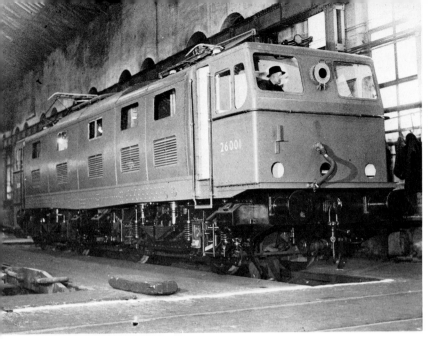

Plate 213 (left): By the time world hostilities had ceased in the mid-1940s, there was little finance available to continue with the Woodhead electric project. However, in 1946, authorisation for completion of the route was given. Construction of locomotives for the line was carried out from late 1949 at Gorton Works, near Manchester. The first of the Gorton build, No. 26001, is seen in advanced stages of construction on 25th February 1950.

Author's Collection

Plate 214 (right): Once sufficient Bo-Bo Class EM1 locomotives were available, diagrams were gradually introduced, replacing steam traction on the cross-Pennine route. Painted in BTC 'Modern traction' black livery, No. 26002 hauls a lengthy train of coal wagons past Barnsley Junction, Penistone, on 7th January 1952, off the Wath branch.

British Rail

Plate 215 (left): Although the EM1 locomotives were not fitted with multiple operating equipment from new, a number of duties necessitated more power than the 1,868hp available from a single locomotive, therefore double-heading was authorised, but a separate crew was required for each locomotive. Nos. 26017 and 26023 pass the size-able yards at Wath with a lengthy empty coal train in 1954.

Author's Collection

Plate 216 (right): When introduced, the fleet was painted in the then standard black livery applied to all electric, diesel and gas turbine locomotives. The EM1 locomotives were later painted in a lined green livery — in which they probably looked their best. Yellow visibility panels were later added and eventually the fleet emerged in BR blue. No. 26035 passes Penistone, on 27th July 1964, at the head of a fitted freight train.

Colin J. Marsden

Plate 217 (left): Apart from operating the numerous Woodhead freight duties, the class was in charge of the passenger services from Manchester (London Road) to Sheffield (Victoria) together with the more powerful EM2 locomotives which were delivered in 1954. On 13th August 1954, No. 26054 prepares to depart from Manchester (London Road) with the 14.10 service to Marylebone.

John Faulkner

Plate 218 (below): In 1947, the prototype 1,500 volt locomotive, No. 6701, renumbered by the LNER to 6000, was loaned to the Netherlands State Railways with a twofold aim in mind. It was firstly to provide operating experience for the machine, and secondly to assist the Dutch Railways with a locomotive shortage. When the locomotive returned to England in 1952, it was renumbered in the BR modern traction series as 26000 and named *Tommy*, the name allocated by the drivers on the Netherland State Railways. No. 26000 is seen stored at Dukinfield in 1953 awaiting recommissioning for BR operation.

Author's Collection

Plate 219 (above): During the mid-1960s, a number of Class 76 locomotives passed through the works to receive multiple operation equipment, enabling up to three locomotives to be controlled by one driver.
Engines so treated were always identifiable by the two jumpers and
associated sockets on the front end. Multiple unit fitted locomotive
No. 76035 approaches Dunford Bridge, on 18th June 1981, with a train of
westbound coal empties.

Paul Shannon

Plate 220 (below): The decline of general freight traffic spelt the end
for the Woodhead route in the 1970s, and the Railways Board decided to
divert all remaining traffic via the Standedge route from 1981. Two Class
76 locomotives, Nos. 76011 and 76009, approach Torside, on 19th June
1981, with a westbound coal duty.

Paul Shannon

Plate 221 (right): With the onset of mechanised power-stations and the introduction of merry-go-round services, a number of hitherto loose-fitted coal trains were replaced by 1,000+ ton merry-go-round services in the 1970s. One regular duty to operate over the Woodhead route was the Fiddler's Ferry Power-Station trains. Passing Penistone in typical Woodhead winter conditions, Class 76 locomotives Nos. 76010 and 76026 head for Wath Yard, on 30th January 1980, with a lengthy train of empty HAA hoppers.

Colin J. Marsden

Plate 222 (below): Right up to the cessation of electric services in July 1981, freight traffic survived on the line. No. 76040 stands in a little used scrap steel siding at Deepcar in this 26th February 1981 view. Note the protective warning bells on the right which would ring should any tall item come into contact, thus preventing it hitting the 1,500 volt d.c. supply.

John Vaughan

EM2, Class 77

After British engineers gauged the riding qualities of the prototype EM1, when it operated on the Netherlands Railway (NS) in the 1940s, concern was expressed about running the class at passenger speeds. It was subsequently decided that if a fleet of similar locomotives mounted on a Co-Co wheel arrangement was built, these would be more stable for higher speed running.

Initially, a fleet of 27 was envisaged classified as EM2 and later as BR Class 27, but as the EM1 production run progressed, alterations were made to the bogies which considerably improved their ride. Train heating boilers were also fitted to the final twelve members, and this eventually led to the reduction of the EM2 order to just seven locomotives. Power and control equipment was again supplied by Metropolitan Vickers and produced 2,400hp. The construction of the EM2 locomotives was carried out at Gorton Works after the completion of the EM1s, and a number of smaller fittings were interchangeable between the two classes. The 6-wheel bogies used under the EM2 fleet were a descendant of those on the LMSR prototype diesel electrics Nos. 10000 and 10001. One of the most significant changes from the EM1 locomotives to the EM2 build was that the buffing and draw gear on EM1s was mounted on the front of the bogie, whereas on the EM2s, this was fitted on to the body superstructure.

The fleet entered service from 1954 and operated the express passenger services between Manchester and Sheffield, receiving their maintenance at Reddish. In the late 1960s, BR decided that Cross-Pennine passenger services should be rerouted via the Hope Valley line, which would effectively render the Class 77s as surplus, and from 1970, the decision was put into practice. The seven locomotives were comparatively modern and in no way life-expired, so a decision was made to store the fleet for possible sale at a later date. After a short period, the Netherlands Railway (NS), who were interested in some 'new' motive power, purchased the entire fleet and shipped them to Holland where major rebuilding to NS requirements took place. Although seven locomotives made the journey to the Netherlands, only six were actually required for service, the seventh being broken up for spares. Once operating on the NS, the machines proved to be very reliable and became popular with the operating authorities. It is expected that the class will remain in operation with the Netherlands Railway until 1986. When withdrawn, one locomotive will return to England for display at the North West Museum of Science and Industry in Manchester.

Plate 223 (below): The higher powered Co-Co EM2 or Class 77 locomotive was an impressive beast, being basically a stretched version of the EM1. Whilst the EM1 fleet was a mixed traffic type and operated both passenger and freight duties, the EM2 locomotive was purely for passenger operation. No. 27003, later named *Diana*, hauls a Manchester to Marylebone express near Penistone in the spring of 1955.

Author's Collection

Plate 224 (above): When delivered, the seven Class 77 locomotives were painted in lined mixed traffic black and aluminium livery but, thankfully, after only a short period, all were returned to works to emerge in lined Brunswick green. No. 27002, in original livery, passes Wortley Station on 29th September 1954, with the 14.10 Manchester (London Road) to Marylebone train.

Author's Collection

Plate 225 (right): After the cessation of passenger services over the Woodhead route in 1970, the seven Class 77 locomotives still had plenty of life left in them. At first they were stored, but were subsequently sold to the Netherlands Railway (NS). All seven machines made the journey but only six were actually required, the seventh locomotive being used for spares. Rebuilt into the guise of NS No. 1506, the former No. 27002 *Aurora* stands at the Hook of Holland with the 19.30 train to Munich, 'The Britannia Express' of 22nd January 1984.

Ian Gould

PART 3 — ELECTRO-DIESEL LOCOMOTIVES

Class 73

For many years, the Southern Region, whose network was more than 75 per cent electrified by the third rail system, could see considerable advantage if they had a fleet of locomotives that could either operate from the live rail as an electric locomotive, or obtain traction power from an 'on board' diesel engine/generator set. This auxiliary power would be especially useful in shunting yards, where the third rail could be hazardous to staff. This dual-power concept was first mooted in the immediate post-war years when replacement for steam traction was sought. However, the idea was shelved until the mid-1950s when several designs were put forward, including the idea of building a fleet of dual-powered motor luggage vans.

In July 1959, permission was given to construct six prototype dual-power machines. The main power would conform to the straight electric principle, with equipment being supplied by English Electric — the total output on electric being 1,600hp; the auxiliary power plant decided upon being an English Electric 4SRKT engine and associated generator developing 600hp, electric power from both sources feeding four English Electric traction motors, one mounted on each axle of the Bo-Bo bogies. Construction of the six locomotives was awarded to Eastleigh Works with actual building taking place in the carriage works, under the watchful eye of the design staff from Brighton drawing office.

The first machine emerged on 1st February 1962, and before the year was out, all six were available for service. After initial inspection and test running, the locomotives were allocated to Stewarts Lane Depot, from where a driver and staff training programme of mammoth proportions commenced, training numerous people on the dual-power principle. Driver training was usually carried out between New Cross Gate and the South Coast. To enhance the electro-diesels even more, they were fitted with multiple control equipment, not only for locomotive to locomotive coupling, but also for operating with electric multiple units and later push-pull Class 33s. After the six Eastleigh-built machines had taken up regular service, mainly on the South Eastern Section, the Southern Region Board were very pleased with their performance and it was not long before it was rumoured that further machines were to be ordered. Subsequent orders were ratified by the BTC in 1964 and placed

with English Electric in favour to a BR workshop. English Electric put the work out to their Vulcan Foundry Works at Newton-le-Willows and construction took place during 1965/6. The first English Electric specimen arrived on the Southern Region on 13th October 1965. The English Electric batch of 43 locomotives were of identical style to the Eastleigh prototypes, except for some technical items that were modified, and the fitting of a revised bogie. All 49 of the 1,600/600hp electro-diesels were allocated to Stewarts Lane and have been for their entire lives, except for a handful going to Eastleigh for a few months during 1967/8. Although based at Stewarts Lane, they have operated on all three divisions, their main sphere of activity having always been freight diagrams, except for a few overnight and passenger boat trains. However, the complete lifestyle of the Class 73s altered from May 1984 when the new 15 minute interval Victoria to Gatwick 'Gatwick Express' service was inaugurated, as these trains are formed of a Class 73/1, a rake of rebuilt MK. II air-conditioned coaches and a Gatwick luggage van (GLV) rebuilt from redundant HAP motor coaches. The locomotives have not received any major modifications for these services, except for the fitting of flash protectors on the wheel sets, all traction and control being transmitted through the train by the 27 wire high level control jumpers.

Under the British Rail TOPS numbering system, the six Eastleigh prototypes were classified 73/0, and the English Electric-built machines 73/1. With British Rail's revived policy to name selected main line classes of locomotive, several Class 73/1s have been named, and during 1984 a number were emerging painted in the new standard express livery of blue body, wrap-round yellow ends and black window surrounds, together with large BR number and logo. No. 73123 was specially outshopped in May 1984 in executive colours of two-tone grey body with a red and white side stripe to match the livery applied to the 'Gatwick Express' stock; the locomotive also received the name *Gatwick Express*. This livery has also been applied to several other machines from early 1985.

This fleet of dual-power machines is probably the most universal operated by British Rail, and it is surprising that the electro-diesel principle has not been furthered, perhaps on other regions.

Plate 227 (right): Once the fleet of dual-power locomotives were on the Southern Region, they were allocated to Stewarts Lane Depot, London, but operated on all three divisions, normally at the head of freight services. Still displaying its original electric blue livery, No. E6011 is seen near Wokingham, on 31st October 1969, with a train of bogie oil tanks from the Western Region to Hoo Junction.

British Rail

Plate 226 (below left): After operating experience with the six Eastleigh-built prototype electro-diesels, the English Electric Company at Vulcan Foundry was awarded a contract to build a further 43 machines of similar design, but with detail differences. This illustration shows the first of the English Electric examples, painted in electric blue livery with a wide grey band at the base, standing in Vulcan Foundry Works yard during 1965, prior to despatch to the Southern Region.

GEC Traction Ltd.

Plate 228 (below): Upon introduction, the first six Type 'JA' electro-diesels were painted in Brunswick green livery; a colour scheme particularly suited to their shape. In original colours, No. E6006 passes Strood, on 19th March 1966, at the head of a 'down' empty coal train, complete with an ex-LMS design brake van at the rear.

John Faulkner

Plate 229 (above): The present fleet of 47 electro-diesels operate on all three divisions, but their mainstay of operation is now the 15 minute interval Victoria to Gatwick 'Gatwick Express' service, which the class haul in a 'down' direction and propel in the 'up'. No. 73132 passes Clapham Junction with the 14.00 Victoria to Gatwick service on 14th May 1984, the first day of full public service.

Colin J. Marsden

Plate 230 (right): A revival of BR's naming policy in the late 1970s led to some Class 73/1 locomotives receiving names mainly associated with the South of England. No. 73101 received the name *Brighton Evening Argus* in December 1980, and was photographed, on 18th August 1981, passing Clapham Junction with the 06.45 Weymouth Quay to Waterloo boat train.

Colin J. Marsden

Plate 231 (below): One knows that it is the time of recession and general decline in railborne freight, but when the daily coal train from the South Wales pits to Tolworth only produces one wagon, the economics of the exercise must have been defeated. No. 73126, hauling one HTV hopper, passes Clapham Junction, on 28th August 1980, with the Acton – Wimbledon – Tolworth coal duty.

Colin J. Marsden

Plate 232 (above right): Until the introduction of the 'Gatwick Express' services, the Class 73 locomotives never abounded on passenger work. However, one duty which the class has performed for a number of years is the Waterloo to Weymouth Quay boat train, which electro-diesels haul between Waterloo and Bournemouth. No. 73118 passes Wimbledon, on 5th May 1981, with the 09.54 service from Waterloo.

Colin J. Marsden

Plate 233 (right): With sizeable civil engineering yards on both sides of the track, Class 73/1 locomotive No. 73108 passes Woking Junction, on 8th April 1980, with the 'down' 09.55 service from Waterloo. There are usually two 'down' and two 'up' boat trains each day during the summer months. However, during the winter period, passengers have to find their own way from Weymouth Town Station to the quayside.

Colin J. Marsden

Plate 234 (above): Although it is operationally possible for Class 73 locomotives to haul boat trains all the way to the Weymouth quayside, the section west of Branksome is not electrified, and it would mean using the locomotive's 600hp diesel engine to haul a nine to ten car train over the 32 miles between Branksome and Weymouth. This is considered too taxing on the locomotive, and it is therefore replaced by a Class 33 diesel at Bournemouth for the remainder of the journey. On 7th July 1981, No. 73134 passes Winchester Junction with a 'down' boat train.

Colin J. Marsden

Plate 235 (left): When operating under electric conditions the electro-diesels with their 1,600hp are rapid little machines, and on passenger duties this is demonstrated by frequent runs at speeds of 90 m.p.h. and over. Passing Surbiton at probably between 80-85m.p.h., the 09.55 Waterloo to Weymouth Quay train is headed by No. 73103 on 28th July 1980.

Colin J. Marsden

Plate 236 (above):   Passing the now demolished main line platforms of Coulsdon North on 19th October 1982, Class 73/1 locomotive No. 73109 hauls a train of privately-owned aggregate hoppers from the Brett Marine Sidings at Salfords, en route to the company's terminal at Cliffe on the Hoo Junction to Grain branch.

Colin J. Marsden

Plate 237 (right):   The Southern authorities seem to make a habit of using Class 73 loco-motives on short trains (*see Plate 231*). To convey stock to and from Eastleigh Works, a special works transfer service is operated each Thursday between Clapham Junction and Eastleigh, returning with any repaired vehicles. No. 73132 passes Deepcut, on 9th April 1981, while returning with one BSK to Clapham Junction. On the 'down' local line, Class 33 locomotive No. 33045 hauls an empty ballast train bound for Basingstoke.

Colin J. Marsden

Plate 240 (right): New ground was broken for a Class 73 locomotive on 24th April 1982, when No. 73142 operated in multiple with Class 33 diesel No. 33027 from Stewarts Lane to Laira (Plymouth) Depot to take part in the depot's Open Day. The pair are seen here emerging from Parsons Tunnel, between Dawlish and Teignmouth, en route to Plymouth.

Colin J. Marsden

Plate 238 (left): Today, in the age of company block trains and mechanised coal traffic, there is little place for wagon load coal trains on the Southern Region. However, there are two small yards at Tolworth and Chessington South that still receive sizeable quantities of wagon load traffic. An empty train from Tolworth to Acton Yard passes Raynes Park Goods ground frame box, on 14th June 1983, headed by Class 73/1 locomotive No. 73130.

Colin J. Marsden

Plate 239 (below): A sizeable quantity of freight traffic operates in the South-East London and North Kent areas, with a number of these duties entrusted to Class 73 locomotives. Passing New Eltham, on 27th March 1981, Class 73/1 locomotive No. 73115 hauls a train of bogie oil tanks bound for the large oil terminal at Grain.

Colin J. Marsden

Class 74

It is uncommon amongst modern traction classes on British Rail to have a major rebuilding programme to produce a new type of locomotive from an older one, but the ten strong fleet of Class 74 high power electro-diesels do come under this category, being built from redundant Class 71 'booster' electric locomotives.

For the Bournemouth electrification of 1966/67, it was decided that an additional fleet of electro-diesels was desirable, but whilst existing ranks of 1,600/600hp Class 73s were satisfactory, something more powerful was required. One of the reasons behind the necessity for high power electro-diesels was Southampton Docks, which was not electrified under the Bournemouth scheme, but projected to still have considerable passenger/freight traffic for some years. The Southern Region considered it uneconomic to diesel-haul trains for long distances over electrified tracks, and therefore the dual-power concept was most desirable.

At about the same time as consideration was being given to the high power electro-diesels, ten Class 71 SR Eastern Section 'booster' electrics became redundant, and the authorities could foresee a method of saving money if these machines were rebuilt as electro-diesels. After lengthy negotiations between BR, the Railway Workshops Division and English Electric, plans were drawn up for the conversion work to be undertaken at Crewe Works. This involved major rebuilding work, the complete body being removed from the frames and reconstruction carried out from the base. The main electric fittings and 'booster' set was retained, with auxiliary power provided by a Paxman 6YJX engine of 650hp, and an associated generator which provided an output to the 'booster' when no live rail was available. Apart from the installation of the diesel engine, a complex solid state electronic control system was installed, which regretfully was a constant source of trouble. Other problems included the starting of the 'booster' set, which would not operate until main reservoir air was provided, and could not be guaranteed to start at all! The two body sides on the new machines were totally different to their Class 71 days with, on one side a window and four air louvres together with banks of air slats, and on the other side two windows and one air louvre.

After the Southern Region received the first completed locomotive,

proving/tests and driver training commenced, with the result that the Paxman engine did not prove as reliable as the English Electric unit installed in Class 73s. Once the entire fleet was on the Southern Region it was allocated to Eastleigh, with work usually confined to the Waterloo to Bournemouth route. To keep the locomotives within the Southern Region's universal traction policy, full multiple control equipment was installed, enabling the locomotives to operate with Classes 33, 73 and post-1951 electric multiple units. Of course the fitting of this equipment provided an ugly addition of air/control pipes on the nose end. When Class 74s were operated under electric conditions, they proved basically satisfactory, except for a bounce problem which could not be eradicated due to the uneven weight distribution within the locomotive, but once the diesel was started major problems arose and, on numerous occasions, the locomotives were declared failures. In good condition, Class 74 locomotives could give some very spirited running, and speeds in excess of 100m.p.h. could easily be achieved on electric power. Such were the troubles encountered with the class, the Southern Region decided to phase out the fleet at an early opportunity.

In 1975, No. 74006 suffered considerable fire damage and was subsequently withdrawn. The Southern Region's motive power department found that with minor alterations to existing Class 33 and 73 diagrams the entire fleet of Class 74 locomotives could be withdrawn, this being effected from December 1977. All machines eventually went for scrap but not before No. 74010 visited Derby Technical Centre for a possible departmental career, but this was not to be and the locomotive was taken to Doncaster Works and cut up.

The total cost of the 1966/67 conversion work and the subsequent massive repair bills, let alone the loss of revenue when they were out of service for lengthy periods, must have made these ten machines some of the most expensive on record, and it was considered that if British Rail had invested in ten new English Electric machines in the mid-1960s, they may well have still been running today, and would most certainly have been cheaper.

Plates 241 & 242 (left & above): The massive task of rebuilding the ten redundant Class 71 electric locomotives into dual-power electro-diesels of Class 74, was undertaken by BR's Crewe Workshops. Work included the complete removal of the cabs and sides from the frames, and re-assembly from scratch. The first of the fleet, No. E6101 (left) takes shape — this was rebuilt from No. E5015. No. E6102 (above) is seen being assembled; a conversion from No. E5016.

Author's Collection

Plate 243 (right): Once the ten locomotives were on the Southern Region they were allocated to Eastleigh, on the South Western Division, where they were placed in charge of non-electric multiple unit main line passenger duties, together with express freight diagrams, usually to and from Bournemouth and Southampton Docks. No. 74003 stands in platform 15 at Waterloo, on 20th October 1977, with the 21.36 vans train to Eastleigh.

Colin J. Marsden

Plate 244 (above): Duties that the 'big' electro-diesels were usually associated with were Waterloo to Southampton Docks boat trains and Waterloo to Weymouth Quay boat services as far as Bournemouth. The 09.36 Waterloo to Weymouth train of 26th October 1977 is seen passing Surbiton with No. 74005 providing the power.

Colin J. Marsden

Plate 245 (below): Another view of Surbiton, this time showing No. E6110, the last member of the fleet, parked in the 'down loop' platform, normally only used by Hampton Court services. For a number of years in the early 1970s, this train, the 12.32 Waterloo to Bournemouth vans working, was regularly hauled by a Class 74 locomotive.

John Scrace

Plate 246 (above): In the comparatively short life-span of the Class 74 locomotives, which were classified by the Southern Region as 'HB', their operation on freight and departmental trains was rare indeed, but the irregular long welded rail trains from the Civil Engineer's yard at Redbridge, to various permanent way yards around the region, sometimes produced one of the class. On 17th September 1971, No. E6109 pulls out of Woking Yard with a long welded rail train bound for Battersea Yard.

John Cooper-Smith

Plate 247 (below): The Class 74 fleet was always diagrammed to operate the overnight passenger/newspaper trains from Waterloo to Bournemouth, and if the right driver was rostered, some very spirited running could prevail! After working these overnight services to the south-west, the locomotives returned with their empty stock on the following morning. On 10th May 1976, No. 74005 departs from Eastleigh with empty vans from Bournemouth to Clapham Yard.

Brian Morrison

PART 4 — A.C. ELECTRIC LOCOMOTIVES
Class 80

Following the authorisation for electrification of the London Midland Region's main lines, and the placement of orders with a number of manufacturers for locomotives, it was projected that there would be a waiting period before completion of the first locomotive. When this was realised British Railways sought a method of driver training and line testing prior to delivery of the first machine. Eventually a decision was made to convert the former gas turbine locomotive No. 18100, built by Metropolitan Vickers for the Western Region in 1952, to an a.c. electric locomotive. This decision and planning was made in January 1958 when the locomotive lay dumped at Dukinfield, near Manchester. After being hauled to the Metropolitan Vickers works at Stockton-on-Tees, conversion work commenced almost immediately, consisting of the complete removal of the former gas turbine, combustion chamber, d.c. generators, air filtration systems, fuel tanks and traction control equipment. Cabs laid out for GWR-style right side operation were also removed. The roof section between the cabs had to be lowered for the fitting of the 25kV a.c. pantograph and other HT power equipment. Other structural alterations included modifying the bogie springing, and trimming the buffers to bring the locomotive into the desired loading gauge. New equipment installed in the locomotive consisted of two Stone-Faiveley pantographs, a Brown-Boveri 25.5kV air blast circuit breaker, and two mercury arc rectifiers; other technical equipment was supplied by Metropolitan Vickers in the shape of voltage transformers, auxiliary rectifiers, smoothing chokes, cooling fans and traction control equipment. For traction, four of the original six d.c. traction motors were retained. Some items such as traction motor blowers, vacuum exhausters, air compressors, radiator, and batteries were retained from the original locomotive, with modifications.

The main purpose of the conversion was to provide driver training facilities, and a staff accommodation cabin was built behind the No. 1 end cab. After release from the Metropolitan Vickers works, the locomotive, still carrying gas turbine No. 18100, commenced trial running. The number soon changed to E1000, which was subsequently altered to E2001. The locomotive was first put to work on the electrified section of the Manchester to Crewe route, between Mouldeth Road and Wilmslow, alongside several Eastern Region electric multiple units also being borrowed for staff training. Whilst in training use, No. E2001 was allocated to Longsight Depot (Manchester), but usually received routine maintenance at East Didsbury, very rarely visiting Longsight Depot.

No. E2001 was the only a.c. locomotive available for some twelve months, but following deliveries of production locomotives, No E2001 was used less and less, but did visit locations such as Allerton, Crewe and Stockport on a number of occasions.

By 1961, work for the locomotive had virtually gone on the London Midland Region, and it was transferred to Glasgow for traction testing on their suburban system. By November 1961, the locomotive returned to the London Midland Region and spent many months in the sidings at Crewe, Goostrey and Rugby, seldom being used. By 1964, the locomotive was transferred to Rugby and used for driver/fitter instruction, No. E2001 was finally withdrawn in 1968, but was not immediately scrapped, being first stored at Market Harborough and later Rugby Depot. The locomotive was finally sold to J. Cashmore Ltd. of Tipton, in 1972, and cut up.

Plate 248 (below): Little external alteration was made to the prototype 25kV a.c. electric locomotive when it was rebuilt from gas turbine locomotive No. 18100. The main external changes concerned the flattening of the roof at one end to accept the pantograph, removal of between bogie equipment, alterations to the bogie springing, and the trimming of buffers. Carrying its original electric number, E1000, the machine is seen stabled at East Didsbury.

GEC Traction Ltd.

Plate 249 (right): Photographic records of the pioneer electric, which soon became No. E2001, are rare, as it usually only operated under its own power on the Styal line. This view, photographed on 17th May 1960, shows the locomotive hauling an unfitted goods train from Mouldeth Road, and it is seen passing East Didsbury on a staff training run.

Alec Swain

Plate 250 (below): The testing/training specials involving No. E2001 were usually conducted between Mouldeth Road and Wilmslow, at the head of either empty passenger stock or spare freight vehicles. Once the first production locomotives were delivered, they were used for training and the prototype machine saw less and less use. In this interesting illustration, No. E2001 stands at Wilmslow alongside Class AL1 locomotive No. E3001, which had just arrived with a press special from Longsight, soon after delivery.

British Rail

AL1, Class 81

The order for the AL1 or the Class 81 fleet consisted of twenty three Type A (passenger) and two Type B (freight) locomotives, and was awarded to Associated Electrical Industries (AEI), who sub-contracted the mechanical construction to the Birmingham Railway Carriage and Wagon Co. Ltd. of Smethwick. In keeping with previous BRCW designs, as used on Classes 26, 27 and 33 diesel locomotives, the mechanical portion was designed as a weight and load bearing structure, the body sides being of girder style construction; the two body sides tied at floor and cant height by steel cross-members. The main locomotive frame was formed of hollow box section members built up from channel longitudinals with cross stays, the frame being welded to the girder sides which were skinned in plate steel. The roof, which had to carry equipment mainly in the shape of pantographs, was flat and lower than cab height, and was constructed in removable sections out of fibreglass. The area between the cabs, being connected by a through walkway, contained the main traction equipment which was housed in two compartments on one side of the locomotive body, access to all HT equipment only being possible when the 25/6.25kV supply was disconnected. Voltage changeover 25kV/6.25kV equipment was supplied but not used, as single voltage track equipment was installed. The two body sides differed considerably, there being four glazed windows on the walkway sides, while on the equipment side, a bank of air louvres allowing ventilation to the electrical equipment was positioned. The cabs were laid out in BR 'standard' a.c. style, strict guidelines for which were laid down by the BR design panel.

In common with all five of the original a.c. classes, three front windows were provided with a four-position train identification panel below. The Class 81 bogie was based on the 'Alsthom' design and incorporated a rubber cone pivot for main body suspension, the actual bogie being fabricated by welding together box section hollow units. All of the original order for a.c. locomotives was fitted with two pantographs, mainly of the Stone-Faiveley type, the high tension current collected being passed to the main transformer and thence to mercury arc rectifiers for conversion to d.c., before passing to the traction motors. When built the locomotives were fitted for vacuum train brake operation only, but dual-brake equipment was progressively fitted from 1970, additional main reservoir tanks taking the place of the redundant second pantograph at the No. 1 end.

The first Class 81 locomotive, and the first a.c. locomotive for the London Midland Region, was handed over by AEI to the BTC at Sandbach Station on 27th November 1959, carrying the running number E3001. At first, the locomotive operated on proving and driver/staff training trips on the Styal line, usually being stabled at East Didsbury. By 1984, the Class 81 fleet still soldiered on with only a handful of withdrawals, mainly due to collision damage.

It is expected that the class will continue in traffic for the next two to three years, and be phased out of service as classified overhauls become due.

Plate 251 (below): The first production 25kV a.c. locomotive of Class AL1, No. E3001, was handed over to the BTC at Sandbach Station on 27th November 1959. After initial inspection, the machine was stabled at East Didsbury where it commenced staff training. In this view, the locomotive is illustrated from its corridor side. Note the letter code occupying the first position of the headcode system.

GEC Traction Ltd.

Plate 252 (above): By the time the first production locomotive was available for active operation, the majority of drivers in the Manchester area had received training on No. E2001. Passing the enormous radio telescope at Jodrell Bank, near Goostrey, is No. E3001 with an 'up' test train in the spring of 1960.

GEC Traction Ltd.

Plate 253 (below): During the 1960s, the electric network was gradually energised from the northern end, eventually reaching Euston from 1967. On 21st February 1967, Class AL1 locomotive No. E3023 enters Macclesfield with a Pullman special for local press and dignitaries from Macclesfield to Stafford and back, to publicise the opening, a fortnight later, of the Potteries section of the Manchester to Euston electrification network.

Martin Welch

Plate 254 (left): The headcode arrangement of the Class 81 locomotive has changed considerably over the years from 4-position route indicators to four noughts, after the abolition of headcodes, and from two white markers on a black background to the latest modification of a yellow steel plate in the former headcode position, housing two fixed beam headlights. No. 81003 awaits departure with empty stock from Euston on 25th April 1981.

John Whiteley

Plate 256 (right): Once the extension from Weaver Junction to Glasgow, on the West Coast Main Line, was opened from 1974, the majority of Anglo-Scottish trains were in the hands of Class 86 and 87 locomotives. To provide the Scottish Region with a fleet of their own a.c. locomotives, the entire Class 81 fleet was reallocated to Shields Road Depot, Glasgow, mainly to operate freight diagrams but, needless to say, their appearance on passenger trains became commonplace. On 4th May 1981, No. 81010 nears Grayrigg Summit with an 'up' additional train from Glasgow to London.

John Whiteley

Plate 257 (below right): South of Warrington, between Acton Grange Junction and Weaver Junction, Class 81 locomotive No. 81016 hauls an 'up' train of STV wagons loaded with concrete sleepers, on 29th June 1982. This locomotive was involved in a serious collision in Linslade Tunnel on 9th December 1982, while hauling the previous day's 22.25 Euston to Glasgow train; such was the damage to the locomotive that it was withdrawn.

Michael Rhodes

Plate 255 (below): Since the Class 81 locomotives have been allocated to the Scottish Region, their sphere of operation has changed considerably. From the early 1960s, they were in daily charge of Class 1 passenger duties, but today the fleet can usually be found on freight traffic in the northern section of the West Coast Main Line. On 5th June 1979, No. 81002 passes Plumpton Foot, south of Carlisle, with an 'up' empty sand train.

Colin J. Marsden

AL2, Class 82

This fleet of ten Type A passenger locomotives was sub-contracted by AEI/Metropolitan Vickers to Beyer Peacock of Gorton, Manchester, for mechanical construction. The Class 82 construction differs largely from the Class 81 and demonstrates the separate underframe and body method, as opposed to integral construction of the other prototype a.c. classes, the rigid frame taking all loading stresses. Because of envisaged weight problems with the build, a considerable amount of light alloy material and glass fibre was used, the rigidity for load-carrying being obtained by underframe plate assemblies. Body panels were formed of alloy sheet riveted to the skeleton framework. The Class 82 internal lay-out closely followed the Class 81, with all electrical equipment being housed on one side of the machine and a narrow walkway on the other, linking the two driving cabs. Much of the electrical equipment on the Class 82 locomotives was identical to that supplied for the Class 81s. The cab layout followed the standard BTC a.c. pattern, and mounted on the fibreglass roof section were two Stone-Faiveley pantographs. However, locomotive No. E3055 was an exception and was the only one of the first 100 built to carry two AEI cross-armed pantographs. Class 82 bogies were of the Commonwealth cast steel type; the only application of this bogie type on a.c. electric locomotives. Air brakes were fitted to the locomotive with air-controlled vacuum for the train. During the early 1970s, dual-brake equipment was installed and, about the same time, the No. 1 end pantograph was replaced by additional main reservoir tanks. The external window/air louvres on Class 82 locomotives differed largely to those on the Class 81. On the corridor side, two fixed windows and two air louvres were positioned, whilst on the equipment side there was one large and two small louvred panels. During the refurbishing of the class in the early 1970s, the equipment side arrangement was altered to provide five louvred blocks to improve internal ventilation.

The pioneer member of Class 82, carrying the number E3046, appeared in May 1960, deliveries proceeding slowly until the final locomotive entered service in April 1962. When new, the fleet was allocated to Longsight Depot (Manchester) and has since operated to all corners of the LMR/ScR a.c. main line network.

During 1982/3, most class members were placed in mothballs at Longsight and Crewe and were subsequently withdrawn. However a new lease of life was given to Nos. 82005/008 during 1983 when they were reinstated for empty stock duties in the London area, albeit restricted to 40m.p.h.

It is regretted that these ten machines will soon only be a part of railway history, as of the five original production types, these were probably the best riders, and certainly the most acceptable to train crews.

Plate 258 (below): Displaying its original electric blue livery with grey window surrounds and white cab roof, Class AL2 locomotive No. E3047, the second locomotive of the build, is viewed from the 'B' or equipment side. When the fleet was refurbished in the early 1970s, the air louvre arrangement was altered. Note the beautiful cast aluminium lion and wheel emblem on the side.

GEC Traction Ltd.

Plate 259 (above): The Class AL2, later Class 82, fleet commenced delivery from Beyer Peacock Ltd. of Gorton, Manchester, in May 1960 and after initial training took place, and the northern section of the electrified line passed for operation, the class commenced passenger workings. No. E3047 prepares to depart from Manchester (Piccadilly) in the summer of 1961 at the head of an inter-regional working.

GEC Traction Ltd.

...e 260 (right): When the BTC drew up ...plans for the a.c. electric fleet, guide-...s were imposed on builders for the ...al shape of the machine, internal lay-... and cab design, rendering the first ...machines to be of very similar appear-...e, and this picture shows the BTC-...cted cab layout as fitted in this case to ...ass AL2 locomotive.

...Train brake valve — proportional on ...motives; 2. Straight air brake valve ...comotive only; 3. Main reservoir pres-... gauge; 4. Brake cylinder pressure ...ge; 5. Vacuum gauge; 6. Speed-...ter; 7. No. 1 and 2 motor amp meter; ...o. 3 and 4 motor amp meter; 9. Notch ...cator; 10. Line 'live' indicator; 11. ...eral Fault indicator; 12. Train heat ...indicator; 13. Indicator light dimmer ...ch; 14. Indicator light dimmer switch; ...Window demister switch; 15. Foot-...mer switch; 17. Cab heat switch; 18. ...pre-heat switch; 19. Instrument light ...ch; 20. Route indicator light switch; ...Tail light switch; 22. Cab light switch; ...Route Indicator operation handle; 24. ...-slip brake button; 25. Window wiper ...trol valve; 26. Air horn valve; 27. Posi-... for AWS reset button; 28. Master ...ch; 29. Driver's master key (in posi-...); 30. Main power controller; 31. ...auster start button; 32. Pantograph ...reset button; 33. Train heat on ...on; 34. Exhauster stop button; 35. ...tograph down button; 36. Train heat ...utton; 37. Driver's safety device foot ...al.

Colin J. Marsden

Plate 261 (above): Although BR placed its order for the ten Class AL2 locomotives with AEI-MV of Trafford Park, Manchester, mechanical construction was sub-contracted to Beyer Peacock & Co. Ltd. A body shell, formed of a separate underframe and body members, is seen in the Gorton foundry erecting shop in the early part of 1960. At this stage in the construction, internal equipment is under installation.

GEC Traction Ltd.

Plate 262 (left): From the introduction of Class 82 locomotives, early in 1960, until their demise during 1982/3, the fleet was allocated to Longsight Depot, Manchester, but this has not prevented them from operating all over the 25kV a.c. network. On 12th May 1980, No. 82008 arrives in Willesden Yards with empty vans from the north.

Colin J. Marsden

Plate 263 (right): From the early 1960s, the train types hauled by the Class 82 locomotives have changed completely, with air braking now taking over from vacuum on almost all services. With a privately-owned VTG ferry van (with sliding roof) coupled behind, Class 82 locomotive No. 82007 approaches Castlethorpe, on 27th October 1981, with a 'down' ABS freight.

Michael J. Collins

Plate 264 (below): Clearly showing the revised body air louvres installed during refurbishment to the fleet in the early 1970s, and displaying a 'botch up' headcode plate with fixed beam headlight, No. 82007 descends the mountain section of the West Coast Main Line at Lowgill with the 08.25 Edinburgh to Liverpool train on 4th May 1981.

John Whiteley

AL3, Class 83

The English Electric Co. Ltd. is perhaps the most established name in electric traction building, and this fifteen-strong class was constructed at the Vulcan Foundry works in Newton-le-Willows. The order received by English Electric was for twelve Type A and three Type B locomotives. However, this was subsequently amended to thirteen Type A and two Type B.

The main Class 83 assembly was a fabricated load-bearing unit constructed from 'Corten' steel, the underframe portion being an integral load/stress bearing unit, the actual body sides being made up of a skeleton frame covered, both internally and externally, with steel plate. The cab sections were also formed of steel, but the body and cab roofs were manufactured in fibreglass to keep weight within the laid down building specifications. Class 83 bogies were of conventional design and formed out of fabricated box sections from plate steel. Brake equipment was originally supplied by Davies & Metcalfe, but this was replaced in the early 1970s when dual-braking was fitted, by a Westinghouse system. Cab layouts again followed the standard BTC style, the between-cab area housing all technical equipment on one side and a cab-to-cab walkway on the other. A major problem with the a.c. types was restricted headroom in the equipment area, causing difficult access during maintenance. However, on Class 83 locomotives a lower floor was provided giving 6ft. headroom in the necessary areas. Body side ventilation louvres/windows followed the previous type, with four air intakes on the equipment side, and three fixed windows adjacent to the walkway.

The Vulcan Foundry production commenced in 1959 with the first locomotive being delivered in July 1960; the Type As were produced first with the Type Bs following in 1961. Whilst building was underway, the English Electric Company were seeking ways to advance a.c. traction, and several alternative internal fittings were suggested to the BTC mainly involving the stepless control principle, but after much negotiation these were delined by the BTC.

In 1960, English Electric sought permission from the BTC to construct the final locomotive of the Class 83 build with a silicon rectifier and transductor power equipment and, after protracted negotiations, this was granted. Later the same year, it was further proposed to incorporate a sophisticated control system, together with rheostatic brake equipment on the now BR/EE test locomotive. Under the original plan, the final Class 83 locomotive was to have been a Type B for 80m.p.h. freight duties, but eventually it was decided to construct the test locomotive as a Type A. The number E3100 was allocated in place of No. E3305. The basic body shell for No. E3100 was soon completed but, due to delays in delivery of special internal fittings, delivery to BR took twelve months and it was 13th April 1962 before No. E3100 was eventually handed over. The external appearance of the locomotive closely followed other Class 83s except for minor alterations to the side windows/louvres, where different equipment was positioned. No. E3100 underwent considerable test and trial running with frequent return visits to English Electric for alterations and modifications. After testing was completed on No. E3100 which provided both British Rail and English Electric with considerable technical information, the locomotive was rebuilt as a standard Class 83, and refurbished with the remainder of the fleet at Doncaster. The rebuilding of No. E3100 into standard form was in no way a reflection that its equipment was not satisfactory, and the prime reason for rebuilding was standardisation of the class. When the Class 83 fleet were in normal operation under service conditions, some trouble was encountered with the rectifiers. These problems were not totally eradicated until the refurbishing programme of the early 1970s. Other serious problems involved weight distribution, which had adverse effects on the bogie components and, thus, the stability of the locomotives. Such were the difficulties that British Rail threatened to withdraw the entire fleet during 1968/70 unless suitable rectification could be found. All locomotives were subsequently stored at Bury after delivery of BR Class AL6 locomotives, and it was not until authorisation was given for the a.c. extension from Weaver Junction to Glasgow, that the refurbishment scheme was granted. After these modifications were completed at BREL Doncaster, the locomotives performed more satisfactorily, but never quite on a par with the BR built examples.

In 1982, the entire fleet was again stored as surplus to operation requirements, and withdrawal took place in 1984. However, two members, Nos. 83012/15 are still retained in an operational state and used alongside two Class 82s for empty stock duties in the London area.

Plate 266 (above): The Class AL3 construction programme was undertaken by English Electric, and was carried out at the Vulcan Foundry Works, Newton-le-Willows. One of the first fabricated body assemblies is seen under construction from 'Corten' steel in this May 1960 illustration. On to this base, skeleton frame and side panels were welded, together with a thin interior skin to cover up the frame members.

GEC Traction Ltd.

Plate 265 (left): In pristine condition, No. E3026 is pictured in August 1960 soon after delivery, and is viewed from the No. 2 end. Compared to the other early a.c. classes, these AL3 locomotives, later Class 83, seemed to have a large amount of equipment between the bogies. In this view, the air brake reservoirs and battery boxes can be seen.

Author's Collection

Plate 267 (right): Vulcan Foundry body No. 7, later to become locomotive No. E3030, is seen at an early construction stage in this March 1960 illustration. It will be noted that although the body is only just being fabricated, an amount of underframe equipment has already been fitted, this being installed prior to the fixing of any side or body members when the frame is inverted.

GEC Traction Ltd.

Plate 268 (above): In the quest for advancement in a.c. traction, when the AL3 fleet was under assembly, English Electric sought permission to fit a number of refinements to the final locomotive of the build; these included silicon rectifiers and transductor power equipment. The machine also had revised control equipment and rheostatic brakes. The engine eventually emerged as No. E3100 and is seen here at Manchester (Piccadilly), in 1962, at the head of a southbound passenger train.

GEC Traction Ltd.

Plate 269 (left): The first of the Class AL3 build is seen outside the Vulcan Foundry Works early in 1960, before final completion, this view being photographed from the 'A' or corridor side. Note that the numbers are fitted on to a plate which is then affixed to the locomotive body, in place of the usual number fitted direct to the body side.

GEC Traction Ltd.

Plate 270 (above): On 8th December 1960, a press special operated between Manchester and Crewe to publicise Britain's 'New Railway' to the world. Class AL3 locomotive No. E3025 was provided for this working with especially prepared white buffers for the event. The train was photographed at Crewe before its return to Manchester.

GEC Traction Ltd.

Plate 271 (right): By mid-1961, a number of passenger services emulating from Manchester were operated by a.c. locomotives. In this 10th July 1961 view of Manchester (Piccadilly), Class AL3 locomotive No. E3029 awaits the signal to depart with the southbound 'Pines Express' to Bournemouth.

Colin Boocock

Plate 272 (above): The final three Class AL3 electrics were intended to be Type B freight locomotives geared for 80m.p.h. and numbered E3303-5 but, as time proved, the final locomotive, No. E3305, emerged as a test engine, No. E3100. The two Type B machines were later converted to Type A in 1962. Type B locomotive No. E3304 (later E3099) heads Class AL4 No. E3036 into Crewe, on 29th April 1961, with the southbound 'Pines Express'.

John Whiteley

Plate 273 (below): From their introduction during 1960/2, the Class 83 locomotives have been allocated to Longsight Depot, but this Manchester-based fleet has operated throughout the 25kV network. On 27th October 1981, No. 83005 was entrusted with the job of hauling two repaired Class 304 electric multiple units from Wolverton Works to Longsight Depot following repairs. This interesting electric combination is seen near Rhode.

Michael J. Collins

Plate 274 (above): Without doubt, some of the most photogenic scenery in the land exists on the mountain section of the West Coast Main Line between Carnforth and Penrith. Climbing towards Shap Summit, No. 83009 passes Greenholme with a northbound Motorail service on 4th May 1981. In the middle distance, on the left, the M6 motorway can be seen, which skirts the railway for a number of miles in the Shap area.

John Whiteley

Plate 275 (right): Giving a clear view of the revised roof layout, following the removal of the redundant second pantograph and the fitting of additional main reservoir tanks, No. 83012 passes Dillicar with the 15.02 Glasgow to Liverpool train on 4th May 1981. At this time, the locomotive's headcode was wound round to four noughts, prior to the fitting of permanent frontal light equipment.

John Whiteley

AL4, Class 84

The North British Locomotive Company (NBL) of Springburn, Glasgow, was awarded the sub-contract from GEC to build the ten Class 84 locomotives. In common with other early a.c. classes, the builder was given considerable freedom with material used, and the methods of body construction. North British opted for a completely integral structure, using mild steel for main body components. Although it was first thought that an all steel fabrication would be far too heavy; when the locomotives were completed they turned the scales marginally lighter than competitive machines which used fibreglass parts. The main superstructure was formed of mild steel plate; the body being formed in a frame on to which the steel plate was welded. Cabs were also constructed entirely of steel. The lower roof section between the two cabs was manufactured out of aluminium and steel, in five removable sections to ease maintenance. Bogies were of the swing bolster type, fabricated in steel plate. Air brake equipment was supplied for the locomotive and air-controlled vacuum for the train. However, dual-brake equipment was fitted whilst the locomotives were refurbished in the early 1970s. The internal layout of the build was the same as on previous types with HT equipment being housed behind locked doors until the power supply was disconnected; a walkway was provided along one side of the locomotive. The external body layout differed slightly from other classes; on the walkway side four aluminium-framed drop light windows were supplied, whilst on the equipment side two fixed windows and four air louvres were fitted.

Construction commenced during mid-1959 and the first machine, carrying the number E3036, emerged in March 1960. Prior to No. E3036 being hauled to the London Midland Region, it was tested on the Glasgow a.c. suburban system between Singer and Milngavie. Deliveries continued slowly, with the build taking just over twelve months to complete. Initially, the locomotives were used in common with other a.c. classes on the Styal line, basically for training and testing. They were allocated on paper to Longsight Depot, Manchester, but were usually kept and maintained at East Didsbury.

After the fleet entered regular service, problems were soon encountered with rough riding and total failure of the rectifiers. By April 1963, the entire fleet was taken out of service and moved to Dukinfield where rectification was carried out by GEC, but troubles continued to follow the class and eventually nine of the fleet were stored at Bury, in 1967, together with the Class 83s. No. E3043, the tenth member of Class 84, was transferred to Rugby testing station for exhaustive trials. At the end of the 1960s, the future for the Class 83 and 84 locomotives looked bleak, but following authorisation for the extension of the West Coast Main Line 25kV network to Scotland, and with tight financial restraints placed upon the railways by the Government, only a small number of new locomotives could be constructed. Therefore the 'stored' Class 83/84 locomotives were taken to Doncaster Works and refurbished, being ready for operation at the end of 1972. After recommissioning, the original problems were overcome but, regretfully, new ones were apparent which involved the main electrical equipment. Traction motors of the WT501 type also started to give problems, and although repairs were effected, the troubles were not satisfactorily solved. During 1976/7, additional major problems befell the class involving traction motor drives, and it was eventually decided not to authorise any further major expenditure on the fleet. Withdrawal of some locomotives took place in 1977/8, and the final members were taken out of stock during 1980. Two members of the fleet were not immediately disposed of — No. 84009 going to the Railway Technical Centre (RTC) at Derby, where it was converted into a test locomotive and renumbered ADB968021, being used by the CM&EE as a load bank, drawing a constant voltage to test feeder and sub-station equipment. No. 84003 was also passed to Derby RTC as a source of spares for No. 84009. In mid-1984, it was still at Derby. Following withdrawal in January 1979, No. 84001 went to the National Railway Museum, York, where it can now be seen on display.

Plate 276 (below):   The Class AL4 fleet, while following the BTC a.c. design directives, was probably the most distinctive of the original types, having oval buffers in place of round, a slightly recessed headcode assembly, and four opening drop light windows on the cab to cab walkway side. No. E3036, the first of the build, is seen on the Styal line in the spring of 1960 with a test and training special.

British Rail

Plate 277 (above): It is sometimes wondered if all a.c. locomotives were at some time placed alongside the radio telescope at Jodrell Bank, near Goostrey (see Plate 252). This splendid picture of AL4 locomotive No. E3037, hauling a train of LMS coaching stock, is operating one of the many test specials on the Manchester to Crewe section in mid-1960.

British Rail

Plate 278 (below): As the fleet of AL4 locomotives totalled only ten, it was very rare to record double-heading of the class. Photographed on this occasion is Nos. E3040 piloting No. E3043, both with their corridor side nearest to the camera, arriving at Crewe on 22nd April 1961 with the 15.05 Manchester to Cardiff train. The second locomotive has its pantograph down and is therefore not under power.

John Faulkner

Plate 279 (left): With a steam heating generator van coupled behind the locomotive, the 13.40 Birmingham to Manchester service departs from Crewe on 22nd April 1961 headed by the first Class AL4 locomotive, No. E3036. When electric locomotives were first introduced, there was insufficient electrically-heated stock available, therefore steam heat stock was used with heating being provided by a steam generator van.

John Faulkner

Plate 280 (below): Although the AL4 (Class 84)locomotives were all refurbished in 1972 at Doncaster, problems with their technical equipment were not completely eradicated, and this led to their demise during the early 1980s. In August 1979, No. 84002 stands in the centre road at Carlisle with a southbound train of chemical empties.

Colin Boocock

Plate 281 (above): This is not a Sunday main line diversion, it is Manchester Ship Canal Co. Sentinel No. DH26 hauling Class 84 locomotive No. 84007 and various BR coaches across Trafford Park Road, on the Manchester Ship Canal Railway, whilst en route from Salford Docks to the main line, after taking part in the Transpo Exhibition in June 1973.

Martin Welch

Plate 282 (below): Following withdrawal of the Class 84 fleet between 1977 and 1980, disposal of the machines has been drawn out. Apart from No. 84001 going to the National Railway Museum at York, and Nos. 84003 and 84009 being taken over by the Railway Technical Centre, the remainder, languished in various London Midland Region sidings and yards for several years. No. 84008 is seen dumped at Crewe Works in this April 1982 view.

Colin J. Marsden

AL5, Class 85

Of the original 100 a.c. electric locomotives ordered, only 40 were actually constructed by BR, and these became Class 85. Technical equipment was supplied by AEI/GEC, and mechanical construction was carried out at the BR workshops, Doncaster. The locomotive underframe was welded from seven box-sections, which accepts all end buffing loads, and is capable of withstanding a total end loading of 200 tons. Construction of the body was something new to the British locomotive industry. The lower half of the body sides and underframe were joined to form a 'trough' section, manufactured out of 5/16th plate steel, the upper portion of the body, including the flat roof, being formed of a lightweight steel frame clad with aluminium panelling, opening sections being provided in the roof for ease of equipment maintenance. The complete top section of the body, between the cabs, being removable as one unit, gave complete 'top' end access and thus speeded overhaul procedures. Cabs were also constructed of steel but with a fibreglass roof to reduce weight. The bogies were of the equalising beam type, the frame being an assembly of rolled steel channel members to a form box section. The between cab layout was very similar to the previous Classes 81-84 types, with main electrical equipment on one side and a cab-to-cab walkway on the other. A bank of air louvres was positioned on the equipment side, and four glazed windows were on the walkway side. Two single arm pantographs were mounted on the roof with the HT circuit breakers. In addition to the locomotive's straight air brakes and air/vacuum for the train, a rheostatic or 'dynamic' brake was fitted, which used the electric power generated by the traction motors during acceleration, for speed retardation, thus reducing the brake block wear on the locomotive. This system applied to the locomotive only, and operated between certain speeds, controlled by the amount of current generated by the traction motors. During the early 1970s, when air braking became the norm, dual-brake (air/vacuum) equipment was installed, and this included the fitting of additional main reservoir tanks on the roof in place of the No. 1 end pantograph.

Doncaster Workshops commenced production of the fleet during early 1960, with the first completed locomotive being ready for despatch to the London Midland Region for testing in November of the same year, although the locomotive carrying running number E3056, was not taken into LMR stock until June 1961. After several members of the fleet had entered service, a shortage of work prevailed, and a number were temporarily stored for a short period at Goostrey. The fleet is now allocated to Crewe Electric Traction Depot and operate alongside the fleets of Class 86 and 87 locomotives on West Coast Main Line duties. It is anticipated that Class 85s will continue in service for some years yet, and classified overhauls are still being undertaken.

Plate 283 (below): The Class AL5 locomotives (later Class 85) incorporated a number of refinements, as opposed to the four previous production types. One major difference was the fitting of rheostatic brake equipment. Two brand new Class AL5 locomotives, Nos. E3057 and E3058, at Longsight, stand at the head of a test train formed of passenger vehicles in July 1961, only a few weeks after delivery.

GEC Traction Ltd.

Plate 284 (right): When the original a.c. types were painted in the all-over electric blue livery, a colour slightly lighter than the present BR blue, they probably looked at their best and, when clean, made a very pleasing sight hauling a rake of maroon-liveried Mk. I coaches. On 27th March 1965, No. E3093 heads the Euston to Liverpool service past Minshull Vernon, north of Crewe.

Martin Welch

Plate 285 (below): In October 1960, a major electrification conference was held by the BTC in London, and in connection with this event a number of items of electric rolling stock were placed on display at Battersea Wharf; catenary was also erected for the event. In this illustration, a Southern Region E5000 locomotive stands next to AL5 electric No. E3056.

Martin Welch

Plate 286 (above): After heavy overnight snow on the mountain section of the West Coast Main Line, Class 85 locomotive No. 85038 passes Grayrigg, on 9th February 1983, with the 08.06 Edinburgh (08.23 Glasgow) to Nottingham service, a train frequently operated by one of the earlier electric classes.

Colin J. Marsden

Plate 288 (above right): With only a second to spare, a Class 87-hauled express clears Class 85 locomotive No. 85018 at Greenholme at the bottom of Shap Incline. The Class 85 is heading a daily Speedlink air-braked freight service from Carlisle to London, transporting wagon load freight in either BR or private owner vehicles.

Colin J. Marsden

Plate 289 (right): The Railway Operating Department endeavour to keep the Classes 81-85 locomotives on freight or lesser important passenger duties, as their electric train heating equipment is not suitable to heat the latest Mk. III stock. Class 85 locomotive No. 85010 passes near Gretna, on the LMR/ScR border, with a southbound mixed freight on 5th June 1979.

Colin J. Marsden

Plate 287 (left): With a splendid array of air-braked rolling stock in tow, including oil, chemicals, clay and general Railfreight stock. Class 85 locomotive No. 85033 passes Hest Bank, on 8th February 1983, with a southbound freight from Carlisle.

Colin J. Marsden

AL6, Class 86

After operating experience was gained from the original 100 a.c. loco-motives, the BR design panel set out to produce plans for 100 second generation locomotives, which later became Class 86.

Equipment for the fleet was supplied by English Electric/AEI, whilst mechanical construction was awarded jointly between BR at Doncaster and English Electric at Vulcan Foundry. When the contracts were placed, BR Doncaster were to have built 60 while Vulcan Foundry were awarded 40. However, due to time and space commitments, the railway work-shops eventually constructed only 40 units and Vulcan Foundry 60. The mechanical portion comprised a superstructure similar to that of the Class 85, as is the bogie design. The basic design of the locomotive was very similar to the previous Classes 81-85, but a major advance was increased headroom in the between-cab sections, considerably improving mainten-ance. In common with the Class 85 locomotives, the complete upper portion of the body-side assembly, together with the roof section, was removable, thus assisting in the reduction of maintenance periods. The most noticeable change on the Class 86 build from their predecessors was in the front end styling, with a flat lower portion and a sloping top, where as on earlier locomotives the complete cab end was rear-ward sloping.

The Class 86 locomotives were not designed for dual-voltage oper-ation, and therefore only one pantograph was fitted, the remainder of the roof being empty except for high tension circuit breaker equipment. Internally, the fleet carried the same basic items as on previous 25kV electrics, but with a revised layout, with the cab-to-cab walkway in the centre of the body except for a small section towards the middle of the locomotive. The two body sides of the class differed considerably, with a large bank of air louvres being positioned on one side, and two windows and two small air louvre banks on the other. Another change from pre-vious a.c. designs was the fitting of axle-hung traction motors in place of the flexible drive type. At the time of their inception, it was con-sidered they would give a ride equal to that on the previous classes, but in practice this was not the case. Severe bogie frame fractures became common by the early 1970s and this, together with serious track damage, caused by heavy unsprung weight at each end, eventually led to 'Flexi-coil' suspension systems being fitted to a number of the class. Modified 'Flexicoil' suspension-fitted locomotives, also fitted with SAB resilient wheels, were reclassified as 86/2. SAB resilient wheels are deigned by Svenska Aktiebolaget Bromsregulator of Sweden and are internally rubber-cushioned — thus reducing track forces.

Machines retaining their original bogie equipment, and now restricted to 80m.p.h. became Class 86/0. In the late 1970s, further modifications were carried out including the fitting of some Class 86/0s with SAB resilient wheels, but not 'Flexicoil' suspension. This permitted the speed to be increased to 100m.p.h., and these machines were reclassified 86/3.

Three Class 86s became the 'guinea pigs' for testing equipment to be installed in the Class 87 build of the mid-1970s, and these modifications included new bogies, fully spring-borne traction motors, and much re-vised internal equipment; these locomotives were reclassified 86/1.

During 1984, a further sub-class was formed — Class 86/4 — these being Class 86/0 and 86/3 locomotives that are receiving flexicoil suspension, SAB wheels, and push-pull decoders.

After a BR decision to reintroduce its naming policy, the passenger-designated Class 86 locomotives have all received names, and it is under-stood that those destined for East Anglia will also be named. All Class 86s are allocated to Willesden Depot.

Plate 291 (right): Two Class AL6 locomotives stand at Euston on 20th August 1966, soon after 25kV electric traction commenced operation from the terminus. On the left, No. E3188 prepares to depart with a Liverpool service while, on the right. No. E3165 leads the Manchester Pullman. When this photograph was taken, small yellow warning panels had been added to the locomotives.

John Cooper-Smith

Plate 292 (below right): With the elimination of steam power and the general modernisation of the railways, the complete freight system was changed, which included the introduction of block Freightliner trains, carrying large quantities of goods in sealed containers between specially-built terminals. Class AL6 locomotive No. E3148 departs from Willesden Yard, on 27th March 1967, with a test formation bound for Birmingham.

Author's Collection

Plate 290 (below): Although based on the prototype classes, the second generation 25kV a.c. electrics incorporated radical departures from previous a.c. electric policy. The 100 strong AL6 fleet (later Class 86) was constructed jointly by BR at Doncaster, and English Electric at Vulcan Foundry. No. E3164, illustrated, is painted in electric blue with the lion and wheel emblem, being one of the first Vulcan machines to be delivered, in September 1965.

GEC Traction Ltd.

Plate 293 (left): After the AL6 fleet was delivered, a number of special test and trial formations were operated to evaluate equipment. No. E3161 was fitted with water spray equipment to simulate wheel slip, a problem with the fleet as no automatic wheel slip protection equipment was fitted. No. E3161 is pictured near Crewe, in January 1966, whilst undergoing tests.

Author's Collection

Plate 294 (below): Painted in blue livery with a full yellow warning end, but still sporting the lion and wheel crest on its side, No. E3178 stands at Manchester (Piccadilly) in 1968 before departing to the carriage sidings with empty stock off the 'down' Manchester Pullman. The buffer beam equipment on Class 86 locomotives consists of a central draw hook with vacuum main reservoir and brake pipes either side, the electric train heating jumper/socket being mounted adjacent to the buffers.

Colin J. Marsden

Plate 295 (right): Although Crewe Works only built the Class 87 electrics, the Works has always been responsible for repairs to all a.c. locomotives except, of course, the refurbishing of earlier classes during the 1970s, which was undertaken at Doncaster. Named Class 86/2 locomotive No. 86234 *J. B. Priestley O. M.* lays on works accommodation stands in the main electric repair shop during April 1982, whilst undergoing an intermediate overhaul.

Colin J. Marsden

Plate 296 (left): After the AL6 locomotives had been in service for only a short period, problems were encountered with the locomotives' ride, attributed to the nose-suspended traction motors; the bogies were also blamed for high track-wear. Between 1969 and 1973, half the Class 86 fleet passed through Crewe Works to be fitted with flexicoil suspension, which eased the problems. No. 86235, painted in revised livery and fitted with flexicoil suspension, stands in Crewe Works alongside a Class 81 locomotive during April 1982.

Colin J. Marsden

Plate 297 (right): When the BR naming policy was revived during the 1970s, the express passenger fleet of Class 86 locomotives was chosen to carry names. They do not follow any set pattern and in some cases can only be described as rather silly. No. 86206 *City of Stoke on Trent* stands inside Willesden electric traction depot, the home of the class, on 12th May 1980. The Matterson jack of 20 ton lift capacity is one of four at the depot and, when in position, can elevate a Class 86 body clear of its bogies.

Colin J. Marsden

Plate 298 (left): The 61-strong fleet of passenger dedicated Classes 86/1 and 86/2, together with the 36 members of Class 87, is responsible for over 90 per cent of London Midland Region main line passenger duties. The authorities try to keep these machines on passenger diagrams as their electric train heating output is more suited to the modern coaching stock presently in use. Class 86/2 locomotive No.86207 *City of Lichfield* hauls the 06.00 Aberdeen/09.15 Glasgow to Birmingham train, on 9th February 1983, near Grayrigg.

Colin J. Marsden

Plate 299 (right): With the decision to electrify the West Coast Main Line from Weaver Junction to Glasgow came a re-appraisal of motive power policy. It was decided to build a new fleet of high power locomotives with much new equipment. To enable operational testing of some of this equipment prior to the new build, three Class 86 locomotives were rebuilt at Crewe Works with new bogies, having frame-mounted traction motors and flexi-coil suspension. These three locomotives later became classified 86/1. No. 86103 passes Willesden, on 12th May 1980, with a Manchester to Euston service.

Colin J. Marsden

Plate 300 (below): Descending Shap Incline, at Greenholme, Class 86/2 locomotive, No. 86241 *Glenfiddich*, named on 28th March 1979 after the Scotch Whisky of that name, hauls a splendid array of vacuum-brake stock, including three ex-gunpowder wagons, to the south from Carlisle on 4th June 1979. It is a very infrequent occurrence for passenger-dedicated Class 86 locomotives to be used for freight operation.

Colin J. Marsden

Plate 301 (above): During the mid-1970s, when investigations were carried out into sufficient warning being given to staff of approaching trains at high speeds, a number of Class 86 locomotives were fitted with high power quartz halogen headlights. One of these headlights can be seen in this photograph of No. 86214, located to the left of the right side tail indicator. The train is a Glasgow to Euston service formed of Mk. III stock and it was observed at Holmehead, to the south of Carlisle, on 5th June 1979.

Colin J. Marsden

Plate 302 (below): After the Class 86/2 fleet had been dedicated to passenger operation, and the 86/0 locomotives to freight duties, it was decided that to facilitate double-heading of some heavy freight trains multiple operating equipment would be fitted to some 86/0 electrics enabling one driver to control up to three locomotives. Regretfully the London Midland Region's motive power department are not always able to keep Class 86/0 locomotives on freight duties, as seen here on 8th June 1979 when multiple unit fitted No. 86018 passes Blackrigg with a Glasgow to Euston train.

Colin J. Marsden

Plate 303 (above): Dozing under the station lighting at Lancaster, on 9th February 1983, Class 86 locomotive No. 86205 *City of Lancaster* heads the 18.03 Edinburgh (18.23 Glasgow) to Manchester/Liverpool train. The powerful illumination provided by the two sealed beam headlights is quite apparent in this picture.

Colin J. Marsden

Plate 304 (below): With a rake of Mk. I vehicles in tow, Class 86/0 locomotive No. 86023 hauls empty stock bound for Stonebridge Park Sidings on the 'down' slow line at Willesden Junction, on 8th March 1979. When the cast aluminium lion and wheel emblems were replaced by the BR logo, the new crests were also manufactured in aluminium instead of the white transfers which were applied to most other classes.

Colin J. Marsden

Class 87

After agreement was reached between all parties for the extension of the West Coast electrification between Weaver Junction and Glasgow, it became apparent that some new locomotives would be required. Government approval was given for 36 locomotives, and the BR design panel was given the task of producing plans for a 25kV machine suitable for 'high speed' running, but to be of basic conventional styling, to enable it to operate alongside the existing 200 a.c. locomotives.

The body design and internal layout adopted for the Class 87 build basically followed the previous styling, the main differences being in the bogies, which were fitted with 'Flexicoil' secondary suspension and incorporated frame-mounted traction motors of the GEC 412AZ type. The front end of the body was also different to previous a.c. types, having only two windows instead of three and not incorporating a train identification panel, but having fixed beam high-powered headlights/tail-lights.

The mechanical portion of the fleet was constructed at BREL Crewe, and comprised an underframe fabricated by welding and folding steel, this 'frame' taking the form of a box section, on to which the remaining body was constructed. In common with the Class 85 and 86 builds, the upper portion of the body and roof section were formed in one removable section for easy maintenance. The body sides closely followed the Class 86, with two banks of two louvres and two windows on one side, and a nearly full length bank of louvres on the other. All technical equipment for the fleet was supplied by GEC Traction Ltd. who were closely associated with the build from the design stage.

Braking on this class was air only, with a rheostatic system for the locomotive, working proportionally to brake pressure applied to the train. The omission of vacuum brake gear precluded the class from being utilized on many freight duties, and thus stopped the operators from getting the maximum availability from the class. When new, power collection was achieved by one GEC cross-arm pantograph but, from 1984, when West Coast Main Line speed limits were raised to 110m.p.h., Brecknell-Willis pantographs were fitted, which incorporated an aerofoil system. Multiple unit equipment was fitted on the Class 87s from new — a feature not previously carried on a.c. locomotives.

Since their introduction in 1973/4, few problems have befallen the class. Minor difficulties were encountered with traction motors and wheel sets, but these have now all been eradicated.

The Class 87 was the first a.c. electric fleet to be built at Crewe Works, and construction commenced in June 1972 with the first completed locomotive emerging one year later. The final locomotive of the build, No. 87036, subsequently renumbered 87101, was a GEC/BR test bed, being fitted with thyristors in the traction control system, thus giving stepless control. A unique feature of the locomotive is that it can be operated as a conventional machine if required, or, by having a key inserted, advanced 'thyristor' control can be selected. On trials conducted by the Research Division some 19 per cent greater hauling ability was achieved in the advanced mode than from a conventional locomotive.

Experience gained from No. 87101 provided a great deal of information towards the design and building of the next generation of 25kV electric locomotives. All Class 87s were named in the late 1970s, and they are all based at Willesden Depot, London. The fleet usually operate alongside Class 86 locomotives at the head of LMR Class 1 services. In 1985, further investment was made in the electric fleet, which will result in another fleet of Class 87 locomotives being built for LMR/ER operation.

Plate 305 (left): Following investment in the 36 Class 87 locomotives, the railway works at Crewe was awarded the construction contract. By the middle of 1972, building was underway with the first completed machine emerging in the summer of 1973. This view, photographed in December 1972, shows the first of the build, No. 87001, taking shape, with six other shells in the background at various stages of construction.

British Rail

Plate 306 (above): Although the majority of photographs portray the Class 87 locomotives carrying names, these were not applied until 1977/8. No. 87005, now named *City of London*, slowly departs from Preston in the summer of 1974 with an extremely lightweight train bound for Liverpool. When Class 87 locomotives were named, the BR logo was positioned under the driver's assistant's window, in place of the second number.

Colin J. Marsden

Plate 307 (below): When built, the Class 87 locomotives were geared for 110m.p.h. operation, but their maximum speed was restricted to 100m.p.h., this being for a two-fold reason. Firstly, the track was not suitable for this high speed running and, secondly, as no other motive power was able to operate at the same speed, diagramming would be difficult. However, from May 1984, 110m.p.h. operation was authorised on selected trains, following modifications. On 8th March 1979, No. 87023 passes Willesden Junction with a Liverpool to Euston working.

Colin J. Marsden

Plate 308 (above): From the introduction of the 1984 summer timetable, selected West Coast Main Line services were scheduled for 110m.p.h. operation. This became practical after new high speed Brecknell-Willis pantographs were fitted. To mark the event, two Class 87 locomotives were repainted by Willesden Depot. No. 87006 *City of Glasgow* was painted in dark grey livery with wrap round yellow ends and large numbers and logo, while No. 87012 *Coeur de Lion* received executive livery of dark and light grey with a mid-height band of red and white. No. 87006 was subsequently repainted into executive colours.

Colin J. Marsden

Plate 309 (right): No. 87012 *Coeur de Lion* passes South Kenton at the head of the first 110m.p.h. train — the 09.45 Euston to Glasgow service of 14th May 1984.

Colin J. Marsden

Plate 310 (above): All the Class 87 fleet is allocated to Willesden Depot, but receive their classified overhauls at BREL Crewe Works. No. 87013 *John o' Gaunt* stands complete and awaits departure from the Works in May 1982. As will be seen by the lack of connections on the buffer beam the vacuum brake equipment is not fitted to the Class 87 locomotive.

Colin J. Marsden

Plate 311 (right): Whilst most enthusiasts of the modern BR scene agree that naming is a good policy and encourages further interest from both enthusiasts and the general public, during 1983/4 BR decided to rename some Class 87 locomotives, selling off the original plates for considerably more than they were worth. In May 1984, No. 87023 *Highland Chieftain* had its nameplates removed as it was decided to allocate the name to an IC125 power car. The logic behind such an exercise seems completely pointless and does not serve any useful purpose. On 8th June 1979, No. 87023 *Highland Chieftain* passes Blackrigg with a Euston to Glasgow service.

Colin J. Marsden

PART 5 — DEPARTMENTAL ELECTRIC TRACTION

Over the years a number of vehicles have been taken over for internal or departmental service. These five illustrations show some of the more interesting items of rolling stock.

Plate 312 (left): This former Mk. I coach, rebuilt as an electric power car, is a test vehicle for 'chopper' control systems, and is numbered ADB975808 and named *Romeo*. It is fitted with power bogies at each end, together with pick-up shoes. All control equipment, which is normally housed in underfloor boxes, is mounted inside the coach for observation. The vehicle is compatible with most post-1951 SR electric multiple units and is allocated to Strawberry Hill.

Colin J. Marsden

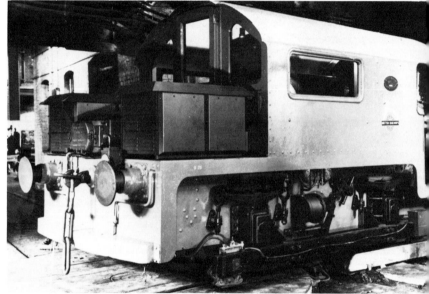

Plate 313 (right): For shunting at the Waterloo end of the Waterloo & City railway, mainly for moving coal wagons from the lift (connecting with the main line) and the power-station, Siemens Bros. produced a BO electric locomotive in 1898. After the locomotive became redundant it was stored at Brighton for some years, and is now on display at the National Railway Museum at York. The locomotive, numbered S75, is seen on the Waterloo & City line in 1969.

Colin J. Marsden

Plate 314 (left): The Southern also operated another unique electric locomotive, No. S74, introduced in 1899 for shunting at the Durnsford Road Power-Station. This locomotive was a Bo-Bo machine, built by the LSWR at Nine Elms. No. S74 is seen at Wimbledon in February 1957.

R. C. Riley

Plate 315 (above): With the introduction of a number of electrification schemes during the late 1970s/early 1980s, motive power was required for these lines whilst under construction, and as a number of the routes involved tunnel sections, diesel power was not suitable. A fleet of battery-electric locomotives was therefore introduced, rebuilt from redundant Class 501 driving cars, each vehicle having its front end altered and a flat roof fitted, traction batteries being positioned in the former seating bays. The battery electric cars usually operate in semi-permanently coupled pairs and can produce a total of 1,080hp. A twin set, comprising cars LDB975407 and LDB975408, is illustrated.

British Rail

Plate 316 (below): In 1958, a most unusual development in electric traction took place. BR Works at Derby and Cowlairs built a two coach electric unit resembling a diesel multiple unit of the period, power coming from traction batteries housed in underslung boxes between the bogies. One vehicle, on the right in this illustration, was fitted with two electric traction motors for propulsion. The two car set, comprising cars SC79998 and SC79999, was allocated to Aberdeen and used on the Ballater branch from mid-1958.

British Rail

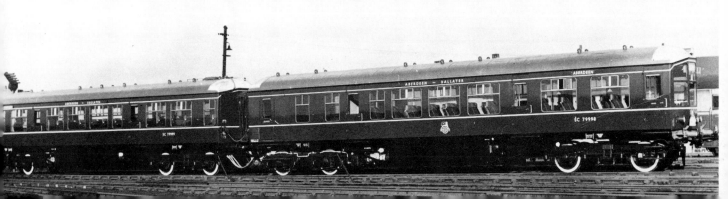

PART 6 — LONDON TRANSPORT STOCK

Whilst this book is, of course, dedicated to Electric Traction that has operated on BR, and its constituent companies, the following four pages depict views of the London Underground, which has been an operator of electric traction since 1890 when the Central and South London Railway opened.

During the following years, a number of London's railways were formed which eventually led to the commencement of the Underground Electric Railway in 1902, the London Electric Railway in 1910, and the London Passenger Transport Board in 1933. From railway nationalisation in 1948, the LPTB became the London Transport Executive, which changed in 1963 to the London Transport Board, and from 1984 to the London Regional Transport Board.

Like the development of BR electrics, Underground electric stock has changed considerably over the years, and a vast number of different electric trains have operated on the London Transport system — far too many to include in this project, but a small sample of interesting items has been included.

Plate 317 (above): In 1923, a number of 'standard' stock underground vehicles, usually formed into five car formations were introduced. The trains, with a power car at each end, powered by Metropolitan-Vickers traction motors, were augmented in 1925 to six car formations by the addition of a control trailer, and altered again in 1926 to seven cars. A six car unit, operating on the Bakerloo line, stands at Edgware Road Depot in 1925; motor car No. 564 is leading.

Author's Collection

Plate 319 (above right): In 1931, 9 eight car sets were introduced on the Metropolitan Railway, classified as MW and built by Birmingham Railway Carriage & Wagon Company with power/control equipment supplied by GEC. Each unit made up of two sets, formed Driving Motor, Trailer, Trailer, and Driving Control Trailer. An eight car formation with Driving Motor No. 258 leading, is seen at Neasden Depot in 1932.

Author's Collection

Plate 318 (left): For use on the Metropolitan Railway line between Baker Street and Watford/Rickmansworth, 3 seven car trains were introduced from 1929, being formed of six motor cars (Nos. 206-11) with five former steam trailers between. It was also possible to operate two motor cars with three or four trailers if required. These motor cars, classified MV, were rebuilt into 'T' stock from 1935, when air brake equipment was also installed in place of vacuum equipment hitherto fitted.

Author's Collection

Plate 320 (right): Between 1921 and 1923, Metropolitan-Vickers built twenty Bo-Bo electric locomotives for the Metropolitan Railway, who operated locomotive-hauled trains on its London to Watford route until 1962, when unit formations took over. The majority of the locomotives were then scrapped, but some went to service stock and were used until the early 1970s. One locomotive, No. 12 *Sarah Siddons*, was retained by London Transport and is now repainted in London Transport maroon livery, and has, in recent years, been available for special enthusiast trains over BR electrified tracks. In May 1983, the locomotive was displayed at Eastleigh Depot's Open Day, operating to and from London Transport under its own power. In this picture, the locomotive is seen passing Woking hauling 4SUB unit No. 4732 (in green livery) on 31st May 1983, the SR unit being provided to supply air as the compressors on No. 12 were unable to operate from the SR Bournemouth line voltage.

Colin J. Marsden

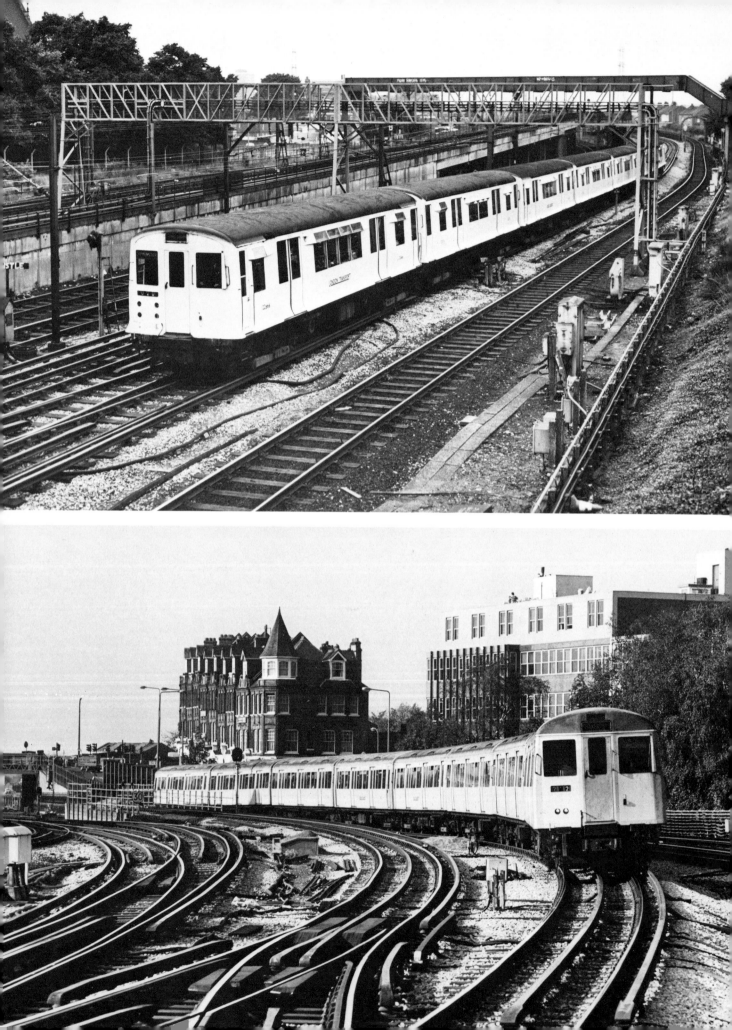

Plate 323 (left): This photograph serves as a good comparison between 'tube' and 'surface' stock. On the left, a train of Metro-Cammell built 1973 stock, used on the Piccadilly line, awaits the signal to pull out of the change end sidings at Rayners Lane, on 20th October 1983, with a train bound for Arnos Grove, while a formation of A62 stock passes by with a Metropolitan line train from Uxbridge to Baker Street.

Colin J. Marsden

Plate 324 (below): The cross-London Central line which links Ealing/West Ruislip with Hainault and Epping is operated by 1962 Metro-Cammell stock. In this view one of the driving motor cars (DM) is seen. These vehicles weigh 26.62 tons, are 52ft. 2in. in length, and can seat 42 passengers. The livery is LT silver with the words 'London Transport' displayed on the side in red.

Colin J. Marsden

Plate 321 (left): London Transport 'R' stock was introduced in April 1950 on the District line. The class comprised several varieties of vehicles, built and converted over a period of ten years. In March 1983, the last 'R' stock formation was withdrawn from service, and during its final years, stock was formed into six car (west) and two car (east) units. On 8th August 1981, a formation of 'R' stock arrives at Barking, led by car No. 22660, with a Wimbledon to Upminster service.

Colin J. Marsden

Plate 322 (below left): The Metropolitan line from London to Uxbridge, Amersham, Chesham and Watford is, today, operated by A60/62 stock, which was introduced from 1961. These trains are formed into four car formations, and normally two sets are used together, the stock being built by Cravens Ltd. A train of A62 stock arrives at Harrow-on-the-Hill from Uxbridge on 20th October 1983.

Colin J. Marsden

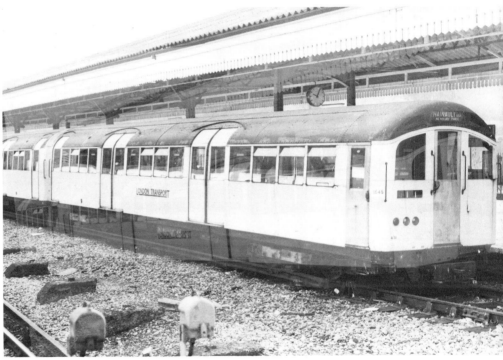

Plate 325 (left): As replacement for the aged 'R' stock on the District line, new 'D' stock was introduced from 1979, 'D' stock being formed in three car sets, two operating together to form a train. These units were the first on London Transport to have single leaf sliding doors (four each side of each coach) which were controllable by the passengers. A train of 'D' stock approaches Dagenham East on 8th August 1981 with an Upminster to Wimbledon service.

Colin J. Marsden

PART 7 — TYNE & WEAR METRO

The idea of a Tyne & Wear, or Newcastle suburban, Metro was first mooted in the late 1960s, when a document proposed significant investment in a public transport system with its own railway network.

The system, with a total route mileage of 35, was constructed in the 1970/80s, with the first section between South Gosforth and Haymarket opening in August 1980, some 27 miles being former BR-owned lines and the remaining eight, half underground, providing accessibility in central Newcastle.

A new Queen Elizabeth II bridge was built between Newcastle and Gateshead to improve the cross-Tyne connection. Although the Metro is considered as one railway, there are actually four separate lines operated: No. 1, Bank Foot to South Shields; No. 2, Benton to Heworth; No. 3, St. James to Heworth; No. 4, St. James to North Shields. All services are operated by a fleet of six axle twin articulated units collecting 1,500 volt d.c. power from overhead wire equipment. Each twin unit, built by Metro-Cammell, is 91ft. 3in. in length, weighs 38.3 tons, and can accommodate 84 passengers, with passenger access by swing plug double-leaf doors. The trains are all single-manned, and operate an approximate three minute service in the 'Inner City' section.

Plate 326 (above): The Tyne & Wear Metro has never had so much attention. Four Railway Club members observe the arrival at Byker of a Heworth-bound service on 15th May 1983. The maximum speed of the Metro is 50m.p.h., and with the rapid acceleration of these trains, this speed can easily be reached on some sections.

Colin J. Marsden

Plate 327 (left): All production Metro cars are of identical design. No buffers are provided, all buffing forces being transmitted by a central tightlock coupling which is fully automatic, coupling/uncoupling being controlled by the driver. Other front end equipment consists of two light blocks housing head and tail indicators. Cars No. 4011 and 4047 stand side by side at Byker in 1983.

Colin J. Marsden

Plate 328 (above): The majority of Tyne & Wear stations have been completely rebuilt for the present railway, but some on the Heworth to St. James, via North Shields, line retain their 'olde worlde' charm. A four car Tyne & Wear train, with car No. 4071 leading, arrives at Tynemouth with a service bound for St. James.

Colin J. Marsden

Plate 329 (right): Such is the intensity of the passenger service on the Inner City sections of the line, that during peak periods trains operate with between two to three minutes headway, providing a far better service than BR could ever have hoped to offer. A Heworth to St. James train arrives at South Gosforth on 14th March 1983. All Metro cars are housed at a depot in the triangle of lines between South Gosforth, Regent Centre and Longbenton.

Colin J. Marsden

PART 8 — GLASGOW UNDERGROUND SYSTEM

The Glasgow Underground was opened in 1896 as a cable-hauled system. It was electrified with third rail 600 volt d.c. in 1935 using rebuilt original rolling stock. The original track plan consisted of two concentric circles each 6½ miles long with no pointwork. Cars were raised to ground level for maintenance purposes by means of a hoist. The track gauge was only 4ft. and the tunnels were 11ft. in diameter, compared with 12ft. of the London Underground. All fifteen stations on the line were equipped with central island platforms, leading to the persistent but unfounded story that this allowed Glasgow Corporation, who owned the system, not to paint the sides of the cars further from the platform edge as these could not be seen! The system operated from Buchanan Street — St. Enoch — Govan — Hillhead and back to Buchanan Street.

Approval for modernisation of the system was finally given in 1974, with closure of the line to enable work to be carried out; the system reopened to the public in 1980. Modernisation was under the control of Strathclyde Passenger Executive and among the more notable station works was the construction of side platforms at the busier locations to segregate 'inner' and 'outer' rail passengers, abandonment of Merkland Street Station and its replacement by Patrick for inter-change with British Rail, installation of escalators at nine stations, and a travelator linking Buchanan Street with British Rail's Queen Street Station. A ramp was provided to enable trains to reach Broomloan Depot at Govan in the conventional manner so that service frequencies could be varied at different periods of the day, and to enable trains to be stabled in the depot at night rather than being left in the tunnels.

New trains were provided by Metro-Cammell, and all were of the same type — driving motor with accommodation for 34 seated passengers. A total of 33 cars was built for the system, all being single ended, two being coupled back to back for public service. The maximum service speed of trains is 33m.p.h. and a complete 'circuit' is achieved in just twenty two minutes. Since no passenger will travel more than half the circuit on the 'Clockwork Orange', as the system has become known because of the colour of the stock, average journey length is just 1.8 miles. Present usage is 12 million passenger journeys per annum.

A form of Automatic Train Operation (ATO) is used. Beacons, mounted between the rails, are interrogated by train-borne equipment, and up to ten command signals can be passed to the train. These include three separate speed limit commands, three braking commands, start-permit, and maximum speed commands. Trains are driven manually between the depot and the first station (Govan on the outer circle. Ibrox on the inner), but in normal automatic running, the driver merely depresses the two 'start' buttons. There is also a conventional automatic block signalling system; any signal can be held at red by the train controllers for regulating purposes or emergencies.

Plate 330 (right): On 22nd August 1980, a two car set of 'Clockwork Orange' stock stands at Buchanan Street. The large 'No. 16' in the train operator's window is the reporting number. Headlight and rear markers are fitted on car ends and passenger access is by two pairs of twin-leaf sliding doors on each car.

John Glover

Plate 331 (left): Ibrox, one of the busiest stations on the line, was re-equipped with side platforms when modernisation of the line took place, thus reducing congestion on the island platform during busy periods. Trains Nos. 12 and 6 pass on 22nd August 1980.

John Glover

Plate 332 (right): Other applications of electric traction in Britain include the 1¾ mile long Volk's Electric Railway, which runs from Palace Pier to Black Rock in Brighton, and which first opened in 1883. Nine single cars operate the service during the summer months, with power at 120/130 volt d.c. collected via a centre contact rail. In this view, a car approaches Black Rock with a 'down' working from Palace Pier, the driver in his flat hat and great coat having hold of the brake wheel. The only protection offered from the weather is the small roof and sliding door.

John Vaughan

Plate 333 (below): One of the most unusual entries in this book must surely be this works Traversa locomotive at Derby (Litchurch Lane) Works, which is used to move bogies and wagons in the Works complex; power being collected by trolley arms. The 'locomotive' illustrated carries the number 2337, and was built by the Works in 1922.

Colin J. Marsden

PART 10 — THE FUTURE . . .

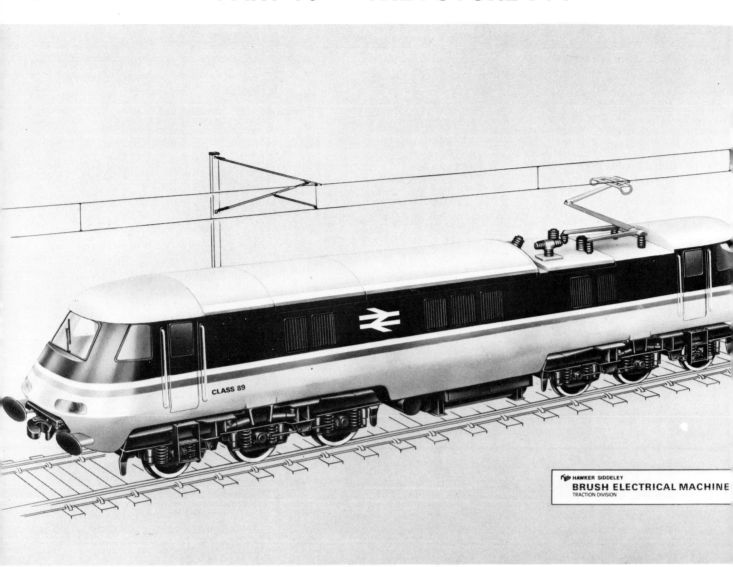

CLASS 89

HAWKER SIDDELEY
BRUSH ELECTRICAL MACHINE
TRACTION DIVISION

Plate 334 (above): During 1983/4, the next generation of electric locomotives was on the drawing board and, indeed, in July 1984, construction of some components commenced at BREL Crewe. The locomotive designated Class 89 will be built jointly between Brush Traction and British Rail. The drawing shown is likely to be revised before production. In 1985, several other electric projects were put forward, which will provide interest in electric traction for many years to come.
Brush Electric Machines

Plate 335 (left): In 1974, the Research & Development Division at Derby built an experimental magnetically levitated vehicle, in connection with a project to study magnetic suspension technology. This project eventually received recognition and served as the prototype for the Birmingham Airport MAG-LEV system. In this view MAG-LEV is seen in its 'flight' mode on the Derby test track.
Colin J. Marsden